MW01089398

Data Strategy and the Enterprise Data Executive

Ensuring that Business and IT Are in Synch in the Post-Big Data Era

Peter Aiken
Todd Harbour

Foreword by Micheline Casey

Technics Publications

Published by:

2 Lindsley Road
Basking Ridge, NJ 07920 USA

https://www.TechnicsPub.com

Cover design by Mike Kirby

Edited by Juanita Billings and Hailey Foglio

First Printing 2017
Copyright © 2017 by Peter Aiken and Todd Harbour

ISBN, print ed.	9781634622172
ISBN, Kindle ed.	9781634622189
ISBN, ePub ed.	9781634622196
ISBN, PDF ed.	9781634622202

Library of Congress Control Number: 2017933053

To Clive Finkelstein,
the father of Information Engineering,
without whose guidance many of us would still be
searching.

Contents

Acknowledgements   1

Foreword by Micheline Casey, Chief Data Officer   3

Introduction: Why Does Your Organization Need a Data Strategy?   9

Preface: Making More Use of Data   15

CHAPTER 1: Data Strategy Supports Organizational Strategy   19
  What is Strategy?   19
  Strategy in Action   23
  What Is Data Strategy?   27
  Focusing Data Governance with Data Strategy   30
  Three Elements of Strategy   33
  Conversations & Language of Data Strategy   39
  Data Strategy Supports Organizational Strategy   41
  Data Security Collaboration   42

CHAPTER 2: Data Strategy is Necessary for Effective Data
  Governance   47
  Data Is Not the New Oil   49
  The Post-Big Data Era   52
  Big Data Technologies   54
  Motivation No. 1: Improving Your Organization's Data   56
  Motivation No. 2: Improving the Way People Use Data   60
  Motivation No. 3: Improving Data to Support Organizational
    Strategy   64

CHAPTER 3: Data Strategy Development (Phase I - Prerequisites)   71
  Data Belongs to the Business   71
  Three Critical Barriers   72
  Barrier No. 1: Lacking Organizational Readiness   74
  Barrier No. 2: Failing to Compensate for Lack of Data Knowledge   76
  Barrier No. 3: Eliminating the Seven Barriers to Leveraging Data   81

CHAPTER 4: Data Strategy Development (Phase II – Iteration)   103

Organizational Strategy   105

Supporting Organizational Strategy with Data Strategy   108

Goldratt's Theory of Constraints   113

Identifying Organizational Data Constraints   117

Exploiting Organizational Data Constraints   120

Subordinating All Other Constraints   120

Elevating Organizational Data Constraints   122

Repeating the Process   123

Managing Data Constraints   123

Elements of a Data Strategy   125

Who Contributes to the Data Strategy?   127

Developing a Data Strategy   130

Managing the Strategy Development Process   134

Communicating and Data Strategy   136

Maturing Data Strategy Iterations   144

CHAPTER 5: Data Strategy at Work   151

Ripped from the Headlines   151

BigOrganization Develops Its Data Strategy   159

Monetizing Contributions from the Data Strategy   174

BigRetailer Example—Reengineering the Location Data Element   181

CHAPTER 6: The Data Doctrine   188

Consequences of Failure to Adopt Data-Centric Thinking   189

Defining Data-Centric Thinking: the Data Doctrine   195

Why Data Has Fared Poorly   206

Leveraging the Agile Manifesto for Business Activities   209

The Bottom Line: A 3,000 Word Executive Summary   217

Index   229

Acknowledgements

It is not possible to put together a published work of any kind without lots of assistance. We benefitted from our share and want to thank all who contributed, with a few special recognitions.

We would like to especially thank Linda Carroll, Ray Smith, David Lankford and Christopher Ritter. Their insight and feedback challenged our thinking and was priceless during the research and preparation of this book.

We thank others as well for their critical reading, suggestions and support.

- Maggie Hubble, Director for Data Governance, Quicken Loans, for an especially useful slog through an early draft of this book. Your comments were incredibly helpful and reassuring, Maggie!

- Linda Powell, Chief Data Officer to the Consumer Financial Protection Bureau: Linda, your insights keep us real.

- Natalie Evans Harris, Senior White House Policy Advisor to the US Chief Technology Officer (CTO). Natalie kept the public sector/government perspectives thriving.

- Melanie Mecca, Director of Data Management Products and Services at the CMMI Institute. Melanie, thanks for all the wonderful collaboration.

- Tom Redman of Data Quality Solutions. Tom, your insights have always been valuable.

Additionally, we would like to thank Michael Kirby for the look and feel of this otherwise pretty dry book. Michael is an amazing artist. Period. His chalkboard artwork not only makes the book more understandable, but also more engaging as well. And thanks to Juanita for saving us from numerous technical writing missteps.

From Todd:

I would like to thank my wife, Roxanne. Her contribution to this book goes well beyond its pages and into the very fabric of my life. She is the reason I strive for perfection.

Reach Todd at: artfultodster@gmail.com

From Peter:

As usual, I must thank the thousands of data professionals with whom I have worked, played and interacted over the past 30 years. Each conversation has contributed to these ideas and helped maintain the hope that, sooner or later, our organizations will get this right! I remain forever indebted to my wife, Cathy, who, beyond her usual editing and coaching roles, provides the right balance of work and fun as we juggle our crazy, multifaceted existence. In the spirit of full disclosure, I have both a fiduciary and an equity interest in Data Blueprint, a company I co-own with Virginia Commonwealth University. My intellectual property was developed at VCU and then licensed to the company.

Reach Peter at: peter@datablueprint.com

Foreword

by Micheline Casey, Chief Data Officer[1]

Recently, I was at a client site and, during my visit, the CEO said something: "We've worked with other consultants over the years, and they told us we needed to focus more on our data, to manage it better and to get more out of it. So, we implemented a data warehouse, and we're still having the same problems. Why?" I felt both saddened and dismayed by this question. This experienced and very intelligent CEO thought information technology would solve his organization's data problems. Worse, there was no one around him who thought differently.

Hardly anyone at the organization had any understanding of data and what they had to do to manage it. At the same time, employees were desperate. They knew they could do more. They knew that, with more and better data, they could engage customers more effectively. They knew they could improve information technology (IT) systems that were not meeting customer expectations. They knew they could improve operations and develop new and better business models, and they knew they could improve overall operational effectiveness. The organization was starving for data, more clarity and a better understanding of what was needed to remain viable and competitive.

---

[1] First State Chief Data Office of Information Technology, State of Colorado (2009-2011); Federal Reserve Bank Board of Governors (2013–2015) – Micheline also contributed a case in Chapter 5.

This CEO is not alone, however. I've seen it time and again in organizations. Even educators have not fully realized that we need an educational foundation to begin changing how we value and manage data in today's digital economy. There are no degree programs in *data management*. There are no systematic ways to learn about data, how to manage it and what organizations need to do to survive and thrive in a competitive global market.

Some things never change: leaders want answers to business questions, and they learned that data analytics is one of the best ways to answer them. However, what leaders fail to understand is that, before they can perform reliable, sustainable and trusted analytics, they must ensure the data is ready to be analyzed. In short, organizations need to have a strategy for how they want to invest their *most valuable corporate asset: data.*

A decade or more into the data revolution, the results demonstrate that high-performing companies are data-driven companies. Studies by McKinsey, Gartner, MIT, Booz Allen Hamilton, Ernst & Young and others agree: companies that have data strategies have higher returns on investment (ROI), outperform their peers, are more productive, have better asset utilization, have greater return on assets (ROA) and enjoy greater market value.

But hold on for a second. If it is that easy, why aren't more companies doing it? As you will discover in this book, it is not that easy. There are real reasons why companies resist creating and implementing data strategies. The most obvious reason is that most senior executives, data scientists, data managers and information technology professionals have never been told they need one. They have never been taught what a data strategy is or why it is critically important to the success of every organization. A recent review of master's and bachelor's degree programs in data science, business, information technology, and computer science revealed a striking lack of any coursework on strategic data thinking. The clear majority of these curricula focus on how to do the technical, hands-on work, but none teach students how to strategically think about data. Understanding *why* an organization does something is far more important than understanding *how* it will get done. Think of it this way: if the organization does not share a common vision, then people will not be working together toward a common outcome. When this happens, organizations can expend enormous resources to no end.

So, what is a data strategy? It is simply a plan for leveraging your organization's data to create business value and gain competitive advantage. More importantly, however, it aligns data programs and capabilities and sets strategic priorities, goals and objectives. Data strategies focus work on the right things, prioritizing and budgeting data investments and making sure they are in alignment with the organization's strategic plan.

If you were to ask 10 different data professionals in 10 different organizations what a data strategy is, you would likely get 10 different responses, and at least half of those responses would be highly technical and tactical in nature. In truth, most technology professionals do not understand the key components of a data strategy. They have never had an opportunity to develop those kinds of plans. Additionally, technology professionals have never been responsible for assessing an organization's data capabilities and maturity level, and they have never been responsible for identifying and closing business gaps to achieve strategic goals and objectives. Some technical experts, however, may have an idea of how to leverage external data sets for enrichment of existing products or services, but these people are rare.

Additionally, many companies still don't have anyone identified, recognized and empowered to create, own and push forward a data strategy across the enterprise. This type of person could be a chief data officer (CDO), but it could also be another type of corporate officer. While these roles are gaining momentum, many organizations still do not have them, and organizations do not define them the same way.

For organizations that have CDOs or some equivalent role, there is still confusion and a lack of understanding regarding what authorities the role has. Adding to this confusion, many organizations are not ready to change their cultures, become data-driven and follow an enterprise data strategy. More often than not, data strategies require that organizations make structural changes. For example, some parts of the organization may have to become centralized while other parts may have to become decentralized. Whatever the decision, however, the organizational structure must support data and the organization's ability to leverage it to their benefit. Furthermore, organizations occasionally need to produce new enterprise policies, which can dramatically change how people interact with one another as well as with the data itself. Frequently, data strategies have a real and substantive effect on information technology and digital transformation efforts. If not managed appropriately, these forces can generate confusion and frustration in organizations, impacting progress and maturity.

I'm pleased that Peter and Todd have taken the time to write such a meaningful and much needed book. This book speaks to not only the importance of having a data strategy, but also to some of the pitfalls in implementing one. This book will resonate with CDOs who need to articulate and communicate a data strategy as well as with those at all levels of an organization as they will likely be affected. Being a CDO or an equivalent is not easy. I know; I've been one twice. The organizational challenges and pitfalls are real, and human beings instinctively resist change.

Many of you want to be more data-driven and to leverage your data to increase revenue, improve customer engagement, increase operational effectiveness and respond to dynamic environmental conditions. Many of you are still struggling with making sense of your data, understanding what you have, prioritizing the right data programs and keeping pace with emerging technology. It's important to realize, however, you need more than a technical architecture to align your organization's investments. Now more than ever before, organizations need to develop an enterprise plan to make sound investments, create new business drivers, mature their processes and scale their solutions to meet rapidly evolving opportunities and challenges.

At an even higher level, board members and CxOs should begin to educate themselves about data and data strategy. The implications of not having a data strategy can be very costly. Leaders need to learn to ask the right questions and evaluate the efficacy of data and data science investments and programs. Simply knowing data's value as an asset of economic value is an excellent first step. After that, leaders should be comfortable asking new types of questions.

- Is there a data strategy in place? How is it being funded, resourced and executed?
- Is our data being used to support customer engagement, create new business models, develop new offerings, drive digital transformation and increase competitiveness?
- How is our data being shared and leveraged across the organization to improve and drive actionable insights?
- Are cross-functional or multidisciplinary teams coming together in support of new data science efforts?

- Do our frameworks for merger and acquisition (M&A) assessment include questions regarding data quality, data normalization and data integration?
- How does the data maturity level in an acquired company affect outcomes and returns on investments?

If your organization does not have a data strategy, ask why not? Raise the question. Politely push the idea. Be willing to change your approach to data. Data work is grounded in customer service and, like good customer service, good data work requires product management and a customer-centric mindset. Go talk to your customers, internal and external, and ask them what they need from their data. Ask them what they are not getting.

I have worked with many professional data managers who were proud of what they did, but too often they took down business requirements and went back to their offices for months before returning to their customers. They took tremendous pride in their work, and they wanted everything to be perfect before any customer saw it. Days, weeks, months, sometimes years would pass before they would release a work product. In the meantime, though, the business environment evolved. Customer requirements changed and, before data managers knew it, the window of opportunity closed on them. Today's work environment demands strong communication and engagement, flexibility, agility, rapid turnaround times and knowing when things are "good enough." If you have not taken an Agile class, a design-centered thinking class or a product management class, I highly encourage you to do so.

Organizations: it is time to get you motivated to start managing data as a strategic asset. Develop your data strategy, better understand how you could make targeted investments in data and enjoy exponential rates of return.

Introduction

Why Does Your Organization Need a Data Strategy?

Some of our readers are undoubtedly from the corporate world and would find this book easier to read if the book used the words "company" or "corporation." We found, however, that these terms are not natural to our government and non-governmental organization (NGO) readers, so we intentionally use the term "organization" throughout. Those of you from the corporate world, please bear with us. While industry, government and non-profits are often viewed as fundamentally different entities, they are similar in many ways as well. All are driven by their respective missions. All confront evolving environmental forces that disrupt operations. All are overwhelmed by the volume of today's data, and all are struggling with deeply ingrained corporate cultures. In the spirit of compromise, we have used the term "business" when referring to non-information technology (IT) operations throughout and hope this doesn't similarly discomfort our government and NGO readers.

Organizations have been told that *big data* and a new discipline called *data science* will help them address data challenges. Neither of these has produced the anticipated results that they promised. Big data projects have produced the same lackluster results as most IT projects (Marr, 2015). Few of them succeed on price, functionality and cost promises. Additionally, we have never found a data scientist who claims that less than 80 percent of their time is spent migrating, converting, improving and otherwise making their data ready for use, leaving only 20 percent of their time to analyze data. This is particularly noteworthy because the McKinsey Global Institute reported (2010) the country would need about 1.5 million professionals to address these challenges. It is estimated that, by 2020, demand will increase to 2.7 million (Price Waterhouse Cooper, 2017). While we acknowledge the imbalance between data scientists and demand, focusing on only one end of the equation will not suffice—improving productivity must be part of the complete solution.

Organizations need regular, predictable, standardized data and formats, a data-literate workforce and defined, documented and repeatable business processes to be truly effective, efficient and sustainable. The way organizations move to a more desirable data condition is through deliberate and focused use of a data strategy. To be more precise: developing data strategies is the first step toward organizations becoming data-centric and managing their data as a strategic asset.

Today, many organizations do not think of their data in this way, and they consequently develop one information technology solution after another, thinking each system will be the solution they have been missing. Too often, information technology will develop automation with no guidance from the business as to how the problem should be solved. Instead, leadership needs to realize the ultimate solution is a human and systems engineering combination that should be augmented by automation where it makes sense.

When organizations begin to focus their work, processes and technologies around data, they can more tightly integrate their work and better leverage their data to the advantage of the organization and its strategic business intent.

This is not a trivial or even a moderately difficult problem to solve—it has been *very* difficult for organizations to make this transition. If it were not hard, there would be no need for this book, and organizations would not struggle with this challenge every day. In truth, nine out of 10 organizations are facing significant legacy data challenges (Aiken & Gillenson, 2011) and, when they confront this problem, it is imperative they have a strategy. These same organizations, however, are quick to get involved with data warehousing, business intelligence, customer relationship management, master data management and other new business and technology initiatives without having any notion of what data their organization has or how the organization needs to leverage those data assets toward a desired business outcome. After spending sometimes millions of dollars looking for silver bullet solutions, leadership becomes frustrated and disillusioned after each IT project fails to deliver true and sustainable business value from the organization's data assets. The takeaway lesson for leaders is that there is no silver bullet solution.

Compounding matters, vendors tout technical solutions, wooing organizations and giving management a glimpse of what may be possible. When these vendors fail to deliver on their promises, however, leadership becomes embroiled in technological quicksand, which drags the organization down and causes it to invest good money after bad. What is missing from this scenario is a *strategy*, one specifically focused on data and the value that organizations can use to align resources and realize the true return on their data assets. Initial academic studies purport to show that data-driven organizations perform better, are more profitable and retain more customers than those that are not data-driven. For example, Blessient (2015) and Xu (2013), relying on subjective estimates, report firms that appoint a top executive responsible for data management have superior financial performance over peers.

Collectively, we have helped many organizations, including some of the most important in the world, develop organizational data strategies. The reason organizations need a data strategy is really quite simple: most organizations have data practices that function reasonably well at work group levels, but they have been unable to scale those same practices to meet evolving enterprise needs, to make them widely shared and to ensure they are consistent, repeatable and wholly focused on business objectives. Today, most can only imagine what might be possible if the entire organization, its data assets and its knowledge workers were shaped and focused by a unified enterprise data strategy.

We have demonstrated that data is an organization's most powerful yet most underutilized and poorly managed asset. Organizations readily admit they could do a better job strategically employing data, but they have no idea how to accomplish this. They struggle under the weight of culture, legacy and bureaucratic inertia while spending finite resources and failing to realize the full return on their investments. For example, despite the amount of research and real-world case studies, organizations still create "siloed" projects that fail to produce accurate or useful enterprise results. Simply put, data—something critically important to an organization's success—warrants its own strategy to ensure organizations can fully realize its true and complete potential. Once implemented, organizations will set a corporate direction, and the rest of the organization can begin to align its resources to the organizational direction and begin to react quickly and nimbly to the ever-changing environment.

It has been more than 10 years since anyone has written a book on data strategy. Yet over the last decade, we have witnessed an explosive increase in the velocity, volume and variety of data sources (Laney, 2001). At the same time, new and poorly named abstractions have emerged on the scene. Phrases like *big data, data scientist,* and *chief data officer* fan the fires of anticipation and confusion, promising to answer the burning executive questions that go unanswered day after day. Most will agree that, to date, success has been limited. Our preferred term, *enterprise data executive* (EDE), hereafter replaces all references to a *chief data officer* (CDO).

Today, data is growing at a rate that is almost beyond imagination, and organizations are floundering in the face of its exponential growth and their inability to evolve their organizations at the same pace. Put simply, organizations have little idea what data they have. They do not know where it is, and they do not know what their knowledge workers are doing with it. With the growing demand for data security and privacy, it is becoming increasingly important for organizations to assert control over their data and develop the organizational regimen to position their organizations for success and the future. Success starts with developing a strategy describing how they intend to organize themselves, operate and leverage data in a way that adds value to the organization and its business.

Implementing a viable data strategy is not straightforward. There are several structural and, more importantly, cultural prerequisites that most organizations have deliberately chosen to not confront. While the procedural aspect of strategy development is straightforward and easily understood, organizations must overcome the prerequisites before they can realize the true value of their data investments.

Organizations have far-reaching data problems that include an inability to leverage data assets, an incomplete inventory of enterprise data and duplicative data processing, among many others. Organizations quickly respond, saying they have overwhelming priorities, inadequate budgets, an outdated organizational structure and intense bureaucratic rivalries that inhibit the flow of data inside and outside their organizations.

But perhaps the most glaring omission is the lack of a data strategy—a plan to help set direction relative to data and how the organization will use it in direct support of their organizational strategy.

Before organizations commit resources to technical solutions, it behooves them to stop, take some time and define where they want the organization to be relative to data. Is it truly an asset or not? If it is, leadership needs to clearly articulate this to the rest of the organization, effectively setting organizational policy relative to data. They must leave no question that data is an asset that needs to be managed, measured and reported across the entire organization to help ensure the organization uses data to its fullest potential. This, then, is the essence of this book: how can organizations overcome the enormous data-related challenges facing them and then put into place an operationally efficient way of improving data utilization.

<u>References</u>

Belissent, 2015 *Top Performers Appoint Chief Data Officers: CIOs Must Partner With Their CDOs To Bridge The Data Maturity Gap* by Jennifer Belissent, Ph.D. and Gene Leganza with Holger Kisker, Ph.D., Leslie Owens, Carlton A. Doty, Sharyn Leaver, Heidi Shey, Alex Kramer, and Ian McPherson Forrester Research 2015.

IBM, 2016, ODC/EDC 2016 Oceans of Data Institute/Education Development Center Building Global Interest in Data Literacy: A Dialogue (Workshop Report) 2016 available online: http://bit.ly/2mvUbev.

Marr, B. (2015, July 01). Where Big Data Projects Fail. Retrieved February 25, 2017, from http://bit.ly/2lNV9Ws.

Price Waterhouse Cooper. (2017). *Investing in America's data science and analytics talent* (Publication). Price Waterhouse Cooper.

Xu, F., Zhang, H. H., Wei, L. & Xin, R & Xu, D. (2013). *The Value of Chief Data Officer Presence on Firm Performance*, 2013 Asian Conference on The Social Sciences (ACSS 2013).

Preface

Making More Use of Data (A Better Data Sandwich)

In general, three things are required to make good use of data, each is a necessary but insufficient prerequisite, and each additive, building on the previous.

1. **Data Literacy:** *data literacy* (IBM, 2016) is defined as the ability to read, create and communicate data as information. Data literacy refers to the knowledge, skills and abilities (KSAs) possessed by individuals who can identify, collect, evaluate, analyze, interpret, present and protect organizational data assets. When these concepts are applied at the organizational level, the organizations become data literate, as well. Rather than using tribal workgroup-based practices, organizations can gain the self-awareness that a better method exists, encouraging workers to gain literacy on their own and supporting the use of data supply chain methods.

2. **Data Supply Chain:** a *data supply chain* consists of a uniform, documented repeatable set of processes for adding value to data as it moves through processing steps on its way to decision makers. Only data-literate organizations realize standard data supply processes—guided by enterprise policies—provide better, more reliable and more predictable results than workgroup or project-based procedures. The reason is simple: workgroups have no incentive to improve their methods or their data products

once they satisfy their objectives. Organizations' data assets improve when they design and implement pervasive data supply chain logistics. Once these are in place, organizations ensure they do not deviate from the standards unless through formal change processes.

3. **Standard Data Assets:** just as a standard language is required for any meaningful communication, organizations need *standard data assets* if they want to extract value. This means organizations must become more data-centric and, for example, begin documenting data assets using data dictionaries or other similar techniques.

For organizations to be successful in today's global, networked environment, data assets are the raw materials used to support evidence-based decision making. Consequently, organizations need to fund and resource these efforts at the program level— much as they do any other organizational initiative. The cost and risk of haphazardly doing this work always (yes, always) exceeds the cost of standardizing organizational data assets.

Combine these three elements, and one quickly realizes organizations will be able to increase the amount of predictable data products that they create and improve the effectiveness and efficiency with which they can use data.

Figure A illustrates how organizations need to evolve to take full advantage of their data assets: *make a better data sandwich.*[2]

---

[2] Various versions of Keynote/PowerPoint slides of the figures in this book are available from the authors upon request and at http://thedatadoctrine.com

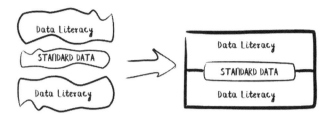

Figure A Making a better data sandwich

Today, however, the exponential growth of data, combined with low use of data standards and low levels of data literacy, means organizations have significant work ahead. Organizations need to begin to invest in efforts that will move data operations from being ill-defined to those that are regularized, standardized and predictable. And as we have already said, the step toward making this transition successful is developing a data strategy. When this happens, the organization will have a plan to move from a condition of confusion, disorder and inefficiency to one of predictability, control and efficiency.

Organizational data challenges are different. Note the differences between individual and organizational access to data. One of the most important is referred to as *legacy*. We define legacy as any system in production. Legacy systems and attendant complexity directly and negatively affect the speed at which people can access data. For example, when individuals access information, making simple queries with their mobile phones, tablets and personal computers, they receive results almost immediately. However, when people try to access information in organizations, running simple queries can take days or sometimes weeks. So, what is happening? For personal applications, there is rarely any legacy involved. For organizations, however, the only time there is no legacy is at formation, and that is a rare occurrence. For organizations, legacy more often impedes the value of data.

Furthermore, when organizations acquire or merge with other organizations—or even simply update technologies, they face legacy barriers that can easily cripple critical business functions. As these organizations become more complex, they become less able to accurately diagnose their own problems. Over time, complexity and confusion mask the real underlying issues leading experts to believe the root problem is an information technology (IT) problem. No matter the amount of resources organizations apply to this problem, it does not go away. In fact, the more complex and undisciplined an organization becomes, the more likely the problem is to resemble an IT problem.

Instead, the problem is one of failing to improve data management practices. Compounding matters, organizations pay little attention to data quality and, instead, first become enamored with data analytics. These efforts regularly underperform because organizations spend inordinate amounts of resources on IT versus investing in their data assets. Organizations need to set well-understood directions (that is, strategy) to guide management and usage of data assets.

CHAPTER 1
Data Strategy Supports Organizational Strategy

It is important that organizations obtain specific, quantifiable value at various points on the path to realizing their data strategies. These take the form of value statements, which must be explicitly enumerated and shared across the organization. Otherwise, the entire effort could easily lose resources and attention to other, more visible initiatives. Before organizations can begin developing data strategies, it is necessary to understand data strategy's role relative to the organization's business strategy. To that end, this chapter answers three basic questions.

1. What is strategy?
2. What is a data strategy?
3. How do they work together?

WHAT IS STRATEGY?

Strategy is the art and science of informed action to achieve a specific vision, an overarching objective or a higher purpose for a business enterprise (Daniell, 2007). At its core, strategy is about creating a default pattern in organizational decision-making at all levels. Whether the strategy is to win at sports or choose an option that results in the lowest organizational cost, the goal of any strategy is to make it easy for everyone involved to make the *right* decision. To that end, *strategy is a literal pattern in a stream of decisions.* For the strategy to be effective, however, it must complement and enhance the organizational strategy. To develop an effective strategy, organizations must perform an analysis of existing capabilities, choose from competing alternatives and develop an effective way to implement it.

A strategy represents the fundamental *why* of an organization's existence—its mission! If an organization's mission is not well-defined, it will be difficult to determine the proper role for the organization's data strategy.

Strategy embraces many different disciplines and areas of business activity including competition, human resources, technology, structural organization, leadership, process and communication. It is a continuous effort which organizations need to perform as part of their daily activities to ensure that organizations continually evolve in response to a constantly changing business environment.

To understand *what* a strategy is, it is first important to understand *why* organizations need strategy. Let's take a closer look.

STRATEGY IS ABOUT WHY

   ...it's not what you do, it's why you do it...

Among many great TED Talks, Simon Sinek's "How Great Leaders Inspire Action" is a favorite. Recorded in 2009, Sinek's talk has enjoyed more than 25 million views. His point is simply: most of us are very good at describing *what* we do, and some of us are good at describing *how* we do things. Not many of us are good at describing *why* we do things. And we can get better at it.

Organizations are like people in this respect—most organizational communication focuses on the *how*. However, focusing on *why* provides motivational insight and several distinct advantages. For instance, notice the not-so-obvious advantage that comes from working in a top-down manner. According to Sinek, by concentrating communications, messaging and resources on motivation (the *why*), organizations can improve quality of communication and benefit from clarity of intent as others design the processes (the *how*) to implement the organizational mission. Similarly, when organizations focus strategically, they can generate well-designed business processes to effectively and efficiently produce the organization's desired outcomes (the *what*).

In the military, the goal of strategy was summed up by General George S. Patton and has been referenced many times.

> *No bastard ever won a war by dying for his country. You won it by making the other poor dumb bastard die for his country* (Wallace, 2000*)*.

In the military, strategy is about defeating the enemy. In the private sector, businesses do not kill their enemies—instead, they defeat them in economic terms. Where the military fights on the battlefield, business organizations compete in markets. While there is no literal fighting, maintaining focus on the primary objective is still paramount. In business, there are two recognized approaches to winning the competitive marketplace: (1) being more effective and efficient than the competition and (2) capitalizing on "out innovating" than competition. (Some recognize successful hybrids, see Magretta, 2011.) The public sector applies these criteria in a similar manner.

DEFINING STRATEGY: CONSISTENT GUIDANCE IN A STREAM OF DECISIONS

To the surprise of many, strategy is a relatively new business term. Prior to the 1950s, people assumed that, if you were talking about strategy, you were using it in a military context. It was not until after the Second World War that strategy emerged in the business world (see Figure 1.1).

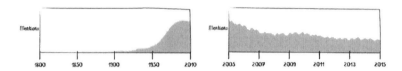

Figure 1.1 Use of term "strategy" has increased in recent times as it is used in non-military contexts

Interestingly, use of the term *strategy* peaked around 2004 (according to Google Trends) and has steadily fallen in recent times. It is not entirely evident why the term's use declined, but it is likely a result of inaccurate usage, overuse and lack of general understanding. If the current trend continues, the term might fade away like other ill-defined terms and phrases such as *secret sauce, walk it back, break the Internet* and *uberize*. (As an aside, Lake Superior State University (2016) banned the use of all these terms.) Even if incorrectly or overly used, the term *strategy* is still useful to our discussion. Liddell and Scott (1999) offer an immediately useful thought.

> *Strategy is a high-level plan to achieve one or more goals under conditions of uncertainty.*

Strategy represents the best and most compelling case for providing guidance to the organization as to how it should achieve its objectives. Henry Mintzberg (1978) offers another definition, one which provides a bit more context for the term *strategy: a pattern in a stream of decisions.*

Mintzberg's definition is particularly useful as it suggests that a plan is action-oriented and actionable versus being something people simply commit to memory to recite without having fundamental understanding of what the strategy is and what it requires. The following statement combines these two perspectives.

> *Strategy is the highest-level guidance available to an organization, focusing activities on articulated goal achievement and providing direction and specific guidance when faced with a stream of decisions or uncertainties.*

This definition allows individuals and groups at all organizational levels to easily learn and understand what decision patterns are and to use them to guide specific individual, lower-level decisions. The following three examples illustrate this concept.

STRATEGY IN ACTION

WAYNE GRETZKY: SKATING TO WHERE THE PUCK WILL BE

Wayne Gretzky, nicknamed "The Great One," is widely considered the greatest hockey player of all time (Sports Illustrated, 2012). Gretzky is also credited for developing one of the simplest yet most often cited strategies in the world. Gretzky's goal (pun intended) is to skate to where he thinks the puck will be. Gretzky perfectly illustrates his strategic approach to hockey as a pattern in a stream of decisions. A clear example of this is evident in a discussion Gretzky had with his father (Gretzky & Reilly, 1990).

> *Father: Where's the last place a guy looks before he passes it?*

Gretzky:	*The guy he's passing to.*
Father:	*Which means…*
Gretzky:	*Get over there and intercept it.*
Father:	*Where do you skate?*
Gretzky:	*To where the puck is going, not where it's been.*
Father:	*If you get cut off, what are you gonna do?*
Gretzky:	*Peel.*
Father:	*Which way?*
Gretzky:	*Away from the guy, not towards him.*

Gretzky's strategy is easy to communicate and easy to understand. "What do you do when you get cut off?" a reporter asked Gretzky. "Move away from the person who cut you off and skate to where you think the puck will be!" Talk about an actionable strategy.

> **Gretzky's goal**: score.
> **Guidance**: skate to where the puck with be.
> **Cost of strategy failure**: game loss.

Strategy can be just that simple and easy to share with others.

NAPOLEON BONAPARTE AT WATERLOO: DIVIDING AND CONQUERING

Here is another example. Consider this question: how does one defeat the competition when their forces are bigger than yours? Military general and first emperor of France, Napoleon Bonaparte, faced many challenges. One gives a classic illustration of *strategy*. The question posed above was precisely what Napoleon asked himself in 1813 as he faced a larger, better resourced and more powerful army of Prussian and British forces at Waterloo (Dodge, 2014).

Napoleon's Waterloo strategy was based on his understanding that armies, when attacked, would retreat toward their supply lines. Knowing this, Napoleon positioned his troops so his army could attack the point where the two armies converged, expecting them to retreat along their supply lines and split their battle line. Based on this military knowledge, Napoleon developed an easily understood, clear and unambiguous message for his army.

> *Hit both the British and Prussian armies where they join, and hit them hard, or die!*

Napoleon told his generals that once the French had defeated the Prussian army, his troops should then turn their focus to the British army. These may not be the instructions you would give to a teenager faced with fending off two bullies on the school yard, but you can see the analogy. Though Napoleon's strategies did not ultimately win victory on the battlefield, the strategy remained functional.

> **Napoleon's goal**: live to fight another day.
> **Guidance**: hit both armies hard, then beat the Prussians, then beat the British.
> **Cost of strategy failure**: defeat, capture, loss of empire, death.

However, strategy itself is insufficient to ensure success. Napoleon abdicated four days after losing the battle.

WALMART: OFFERING EVERY DAY LOW PRICES

A final example is a business slogan that many readers may already know. It is no secret that for many years, Walmart's organizational strategy could be distilled into four effective words: *Every day, low prices.* Walmart's strategy provided continuous guidance to the organization. Walmart realized that, if the company wanted its customers, suppliers and partners to understand that Walmart was the low-price leader, achieving the lowest prices must be how decisions are evaluated inside and outside the organization. As history has shown, Walmart's strategy proved successful over time. It is a strategy that everyone—including corporate leaders, managers, employees, vendors and customers—understands. The strategy took root in nearly every aspect of the company, wherein each organizational component did its part to lower costs and deliver superior pricing to Walmart customers worldwide. Walmart's corporate culture embodies this credo, with new employees quickly learning it and customers being bombarded with this singular message across all forms of advertising.

As a strategy, it is easy to see how this produces a pattern in a stream of Walmart operational decisions. As Walmart continues its attempt to become the first $1 trillion organization, it is hard to argue with the financial success that its strategy has brought to the organization.

> **Walmart's goal:** achieve sales growth.
> **Guidance**: provide low prices to customers every day.
> **Cost of strategy failure**: another retailer gets those sales and customers.

WHAT IS STRATEGY?

Recall our definition.

> *Strategy is the highest-level guidance available to an organization, focusing activities on articulated goal achievement and providing direction and specific guidance when faced with a stream of decisions or uncertainties.*

In any sector, for a strategy to be effective, it tends to satisfy four specific criteria (Roberts, 2004). A strategy:

- expresses specific goals;
- delineates a specific scope;
- describes the advantage sought after; and
- articulates why the strategy is achievable.

A specific strategy is then an expression of organizational objectives that identifies specific goals within a confined scope of operations to attain a specified advantage. Specific strategy articulation should also describe why the organization believes it can successfully implement this strategy and how that strategy will benefit the organization. Many have said:

Strategy is the organization, and the organization is the strategy.

This indicates the depth of integration desirable—and most often required—to achieve results.

Because the environment is not static, organizations cannot expect to be successful doing things the way they have always done them. To achieve new business outcomes, organizations must make incremental adjustments over time and evolve in response to a fluid, changing business environment. Consequently, organizations must learn how to do things differently. They must discover new and innovative ways to manage change both inside and outside the organizations, and they must operate in a way that keeps pace with a rapidly changing business climate. If they do not do this, they will fail to maintain their current (relative) position.

WHAT IS DATA STRATEGY?

So far, we have discussed what strategy is and why it is important. We have also described strategy as an impetus for establishing organizational momentum and how strategy must embody the organization and *vice versa*. Let us now put these concepts together and describe the role played by a data strategy.

A data strategy is about supplying motivation centered around use of organizational data assets in support of organizational strategy. Specifically:

> *[d] ata strategy is the highest level [of] guidance available to an organization, focusing data-related activities on articulated data goal achievements and providing directional and specific guidance when faced with a stream of decisions or uncertainties about organizational data assets and their application toward business objectives.*

Developing and maintaining an organizational data strategy should be a ***primary*** function for an enterprise data executive (EDE). Recall the criteria for a strategy: a strategy includes scope and achievable goals while targeting improvement of the organization's data. Most organizations do not treat data as the organizational asset it is. However, data is every organization's single, non-depletable, non-degrading, durable strategic asset. Consider for a moment the above characteristics of organizational assets.

- **Data assets cannot be depleted.** Data is different from other assets in that its greatest value comes not from being *used* but from being *reused*.

- **Data assets do not degrade over time.** Digital assets, when properly maintained, do not degrade over time as other organizational assets do.

- **Data assets are durable.** They can generate flows of goods and services over time (Rust, 1985).

- **Data assets are strategic.** Data assets must be maintained by an organization to achieve future outcomes. Without strategic assets, the future of the organization is jeopardized.

Combined, these four properties make data unique among organizational assets. We regularly observe organizations managing data assets with no degree of professionalism and using inadequate methods or appropriate technology. Without this foundation, organizations have no framework (policy) to leverage data usage. They fail to leverage data assets per any repeatable and documented process, thereby losing productivity (process). They spend far too much on information technology (IT) investments, but they do not properly implement a data-centric means of enabling their knowledge workers (people) to use and exploit data assets.

A primary lesson is that the solution to these problems is not fundamentally a technology-based solution. No organization has been identified that would not benefit from a balance of people, process, policy and technology (P3T) within their solution set. Organizations must focus data strategy on business outcomes that help exploit data across the digital landscape to create value in the form of innovation, customer engagement and growth. Putting it another way: your data strategy needs to be:

- concise and consume less bandwidth to absorb than the organizational strategy;

- actionable and support a valid and useable organizational strategy; and

- easily understood by everyone in the organization, including business and IT.

These three characteristics combine to guide the organization's data governance program.

FOCUSING DATA GOVERNANCE WITH DATA STRATEGY

A primary benefit of a data strategy is the introduction of focus for data governance efforts. Data governance currently has many different definitions, including the following from John Ladley (2012).

> *Data governance is the organization and implementation of policies, procedures, structure, roles and responsibilities which outline and enforce rules of engagement, decision rights and accountabilities for the effective management of information assets.*

Data governance is best defined as *managing data with guidance.* It is best because it enables the following question.

> *Do you prefer that your sole, non-depletable, non-degrading durable strategic asset be managed without guidance?*

To date, no one has been found who is willing to answer "yes" to this question. Once organizations recognize that they must have data governance, the conversation can address *how* data assets are governed. The answer to this question includes developing a data strategy. Figure 1.2 illustrates how organizational data strategies help shape data governance efforts, ensuring that organizational data assets are optimized so as to derive the most value in support of the organizational strategy. As a further refinement of this concept, it is suggested that organizations use business goals as the means to shape data governance and ensure that governance is aligned with the data strategy. This is accomplished by using the language of data governance—metadata.

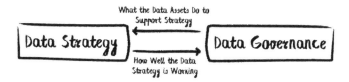

Figure 1.2 Data strategy works hand in hand with data governance

It has repeatedly been found that organizations attempt to implement governance as a top-down edict without fully understanding the foundational concepts. For example, consider the role, data steward. Organizations have differing understandings of and operational expectations for this role. In fact, the same title is used for different roles across the organization. The net result of doing this is confusion. So instead of using overly complex roles and titles, keep it simple and initially avoid confusing titles such as those listed below (Plotkin, 2014).

- **business data steward**: manage from the perspective of business elements (i.e. business definitions and data quality).

- **technical data steward**: focus on the use of data by systems and models (i.e. code operation).

- **project data steward**: gather definitions, data quality rules and project issues for referral to business and technical data stewards.

- **domain data steward**: manage data required across multiple business areas (i.e. customer data) and metadata documentation.

- **operational data steward**: directly input data or instruct those who do; aid business data stewards in spotting data issues and identifying their root causes.
- **data quality stewards**: focus specifically on resolving data quality issues.

Keep the message simple. For example, identify a steward who will own certain kinds of decisions—instead of attempting to define all types of decision in advance where you have the least knowledge.

Listed below are other benefits of data strategy-governance combinations. The following list was postulated by Adelman, Moss & Abai (2005). Although articulated in 2005, these phrases still hold true. The list included the following benefits.

- revenue enhancement
- cash flow acceleration
- analyst productivity
- cost containment
- demand chain management
- fraud reduction
- competitive effectiveness
- better and faster decision making
- better customer service
- employee empowerment
- increased marketing effectiveness
- improved supplier and customer relationships

Other detailed benefits include customer conversion, attrition and retention improvements and better public relations, reputation and shareholder impact. While we are certain this list is not exhaustive, it does represent an excellent starting point for making a variety of business cases to invest more in data assets.

THREE ELEMENTS OF STRATEGY

Most organizations are constantly busy working toward the next deadline. They are focused, single-minded and motivated. This is a good thing...or is it? Being driven by short-term goals should not preclude thinking about the future, and good managers always find time to reflect on where the organization is heading and questioning whether its strategy is still valid.

As part of this process, organizations must understand their markets and carefully balance what they can offer to satisfy needs. When they do this, organizations begin making sense of the complex forces with which they interact. Once complete, organizations can leverage that knowledge and use it to create successful strategies. This is not an optional task; it is an essential function if organizations are to survive (Williams, 2009).

Experience suggests that many organizational strategies are not as effective as they could be. They are often overly complex, difficult to understand, lofty and difficult to translate into practical terms. If that's not enough, strategies are often mired in details that mask the direction the organization desires to travel. As a result, such strategies quickly become difficult to describe and generally ineffective for guiding real-world operations. Strategy documentation ends up sitting on a shelf, unused.

Let's explore three core strategic characteristics that animate and motivate strategy: analysis, choice and implementation.

ANALYSIS

As has been suggested, complex strategies can be very difficult to communicate to associates, partners and subordinates. When communication breaks down, implementation of the strategy is nearly impossible. Wayne Gretzky realized the futility of chasing the faster hockey puck around the rink and decided to, instead, put himself in a position where he would more likely be able to receive a pass from a teammate and score. Skate to where you think the puck will be. So how do you determine where the puck will be?

One technique is *Porter's Market Positioning Framework.* Analyzing the environment in which you operate is the first step to creating a strategy, and, to understand the environment, you must dedicate time to collect data. For example, to be a successful car dealer, one must buy the right cars, at the right prices, at the right time, under the right conditions. To do this, one must spend time analyzing the market, watching and listening for information about which cars are—and are not—selling well and which cars are increasing in price or decreasing in value. This requires careful observations. But, it also requires real data, such as week-to-week recording and analysis of car price data, customer numbers and stock levels.

A tool like Porter's can help one assess appropriate factors. In some instances, it has prevented organizations from competing against themselves. Some internal factors may include marketing, management, operations and production, accounting and finance, computer information systems and research and development capabilities. Some external factors may include politics, government, law, economy, technology, society, demographics, culture and competition. Armed with this kind of information, organizations can begin developing strategies that directly reflect the environment and its forces.

Using Porter's model, Figure 1.3 shows different strategies that organizations use.

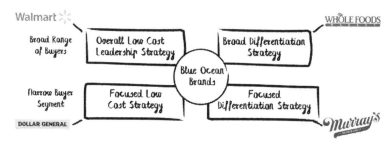

Figure 1.3 Porter's Market Positioning Framework

- Walmart strives to provide the lowest cost to the broadest range of customers.

- Whole Foods offers a variety of items to a range of buyers.

- Dollar General tries to capture a narrow segment of Walmart's customers.

- Murray's Cheese pursues a small segment of cheese connoisseurs.

- Trader Joe's uses what Porter called a "Blue Ocean" strategy which tries to be several things to a range of customers.

This sort of strategic analysis leads to discussion about why the organization exists. What is the organization's purpose and mission? These types of discussions occur well after organizations are formed, and they are often accompanied by statements such as, "We are now refocusing on our core competencies." This behavior is good and reflects the reality that organizations, and their strategies, need to evolve over time, adapt to changing conditions and exploit internal competencies.

Organizations have many data assets. Most have so many they become obstacles by increasing the complexity of the operational environment. An organizational data asset inventory capability is a necessary but insufficient prerequisite to implementing a successful data strategy. Analysis of the organizational data asset inventory will help to assess the utility of individual data collections, thereby permitting the organization to prioritize the order in which they should be improved and employed. Note: The authors have never seen a completed data inventory, so never let yourself get pinned down as to a data when yours will be complete!

CHOICE

Strategy must convey choice, which, in and of itself, necessitates organizational trade-offs. Napoleon understood this and realized he could not defeat a large enemy using a smaller army, so he devised a plan to literally divide and conquer.:

> *First, we hit them both where their forces join, causing them to retreat away from each other. Second, we turn and defeat the Prussians, then defeat the British.*

After analyzing the environment, organizations have enough information to be able to identify the basic, business-level strategy choices organizations need to make. Collectively, these basic choices are sometimes called "generic business-level strategy." Grünig & Kühn, 2015).

Organizations that pursue a standardized or segmentation strategy recognize that they must adjust behaviors depending on the specific environment or target. Organizations pursuing a segmentation strategy recognize different segments and tailor behavior appropriately. Organizations pursuing a standardization strategy focus on a cheaper approach, such as serving the consumer as a single type.

Organizations that target a broad environment can concentrate on reducing costs to the lowest levels while still making a profit. When this happens, it typically is said that the organization is pursuing a broad low-cost strategy. Alternatively, if an organization differentiates its product in some way, the organization is pursuing a broad differentiation strategy.

Organizations that decide to recognize different segments and offer different products to each segment pursue a broad differentiation strategy. It is possible, however, to pursue a differentiation strategy while not recognizing different segments, as Coca-Cola did prior to the 1980s. Walmart is pursuing a broad low-cost strategy, whereas Toyota and Coca-Cola are both pursuing a broad differentiation strategy.

Companies that target a few segments, or more typically just one, are pursuing a focus or niche strategy. These companies can either try to be the low-cost player in that niche, as Walmart has done by pursuing a focused low-cost strategy, or they can try to customize their offering to the needs of that particular segment through the addition of features and functions, in which case they are pursuing a focused differentiation strategy.

Furthermore, strategy must convey choice involving trade-offs. In business terms, a logical next step would be to determine the various strategic choices facing an organization. Using Porter's Market Positioning Framework (see Figure 1.4), organizations can assess and codify factors such as market position.

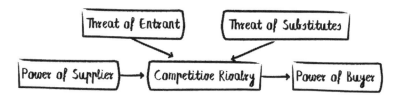

Figure 1.4 The Competitive Advantage Framework

Other strategic choices can be articulated to gain insight to market competition.

- *bargaining power of buyers*: the degree of leverage customers have over your company.

- *bargaining power of suppliers*: the degree of leverage suppliers have over your company.

- *threat of new entrants*: the likelihood of new competition entering the market.

- *threat of substitute products*: the likelihood of customers switching to alternative products.

Assuming organizations are largely aware of their data holdings and their relative value, the choice function is concerned with determining the relative ability of the data collections to support the organizational strategy. While it should go without saying, experience demands the explicit statement that it is impossible to use all an organization's data assets all at once. Therefore, the choice function is key to developing and maintaining a specific focus for subsequent cycles.

IMPLEMENTATION

As has been suggested, if organizations develop an overly complex strategy, it can be enormously difficult to share with employees, associates and partners, and it can be even more difficult to implement. Recall Gretzky's realization of the futility of chasing the faster hockey puck around the rink and, instead, determining to put himself in a position where he would be more likely to receive a pass from a teammate and score.

While this approach may have worked for Gretzky, it is important to note he did not work alone. As part of a team, his specific actions needed to be incorporated in the larger team plan. Additionally, Gretzky had to be able to share his ideas and strategies with others on the team so they could operate as a single, cohesive unit on the ice.

Strategy must be something all organizational members can articulate, understand, internalize and repeat. More specifically, this means that everyone must understand their roles and responsibilities relative to the entire strategy. (This condition is often referred to as *swim lanes*.) Unless everyone understands the context of the plan, members will not be able to function in an orchestrated and coordinated manner and, thus, realize the strategic intent.

CONVERSATIONS & LANGUAGE OF DATA STRATEGY

It is important to note that organizations should not wait until things are settled, stable or finished before starting to implement these concepts. For those organizations that do not develop data strategies and learn to manage their data, they will painfully learn there will always be a good reason for not making changes to their organization and its behavior. This lack of organizational fortitude, commitment and action will have detrimental effects on the organization and its ability to continue meeting the demands of an ever-evolving, competitive environment.

In today's digital world, the business becomes data and data becomes the business, and the information derived from that data becomes the most important corporate asset. To that end, what truly matters the most is an organization's ability to evolve, create, capture and leverage value from data. However, we should note that data is not static. It is not finite. Instead, data grows larger, more diverse and more distributed 24/7, increasingly being generated and residing outside the enterprise and its immediate control. At the same time, the environment is quickly becoming interconnected by devices and equipment to people in both home and work environments.

Taken together, the environment is quickly becoming an ecosystem of networks and connections through which today's data flows. With this as the backdrop, an important question arises: how do organizations capture and use the data that follows individuals? Organizations must focus their data strategy on those business outcomes that help the organization exploit data across the digital landscape, creating value in the form of innovation, customer engagement and growth.

Furthermore, it is incumbent upon data professionals to ensure that organizational conversations about data are framed as much as possible as *business* conversations. Technical experts need to talk about data in a more business-friendly manner. They must discuss data form and function to provide the business with technical solutions to business problems. However, while a valid conversation, technical discussion cannot happen in a vacuum. Technical conversations must relate to the business and, ultimately, align to the data strategy.

When reviewing a data strategy, ask yourself: what business outcome am I seeking? Although it is an obvious question, when posed to clients, 80 percent have no answer, a vague answer or the wrong answer. Of the total sample, only 5 percent understand the relationship between specific, component-level IT work and the organization's overarching organizational strategy.

Additionally, answering this question changes the conversation from one about systems and data to one about business and outcomes. Turn data conversations into business conversations (*why* instead of *how*). If you cannot answer the question, you should not be doing what you are doing. It is never too late to stop projects that are not supporting business outcomes.

As well as changing the subject of data conversations, data professionals must also change the language used. Language is one of the most important tools with which to engage people and inspire them to participate. If the wrong words are used, the audience is lost. If the right words are used, people get excited about what information can do for them and for the business. Use words that express *value* and *opportunity* but that are not boring or scary. Being a master of information management competencies, technology and business value is not enough—you must become a good communicator to illustrate the interdependent business and systems complexities to budget authorities.

DATA STRATEGY SUPPORTS ORGANIZATIONAL STRATEGY

While oft-repeated that strategy is the organization and *vice versa*, data assets are not the only asset employed by organizations to achieve strategic objectives. The data strategy must be subordinate to the organizational strategy.

Figure 1.5 illustrates this, showing the symbiotic relationship between data strategy and data governance.

Organizational strategy provides guidance to and context for the data strategy. Data governance, in turn, implements data strategy through its influence over aspects of IT projects, which exist to deliver data to organizational knowledge workers and partner organizations.

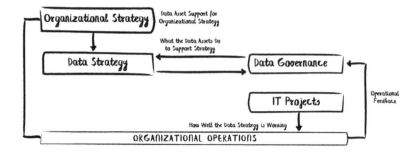

Figure 1.5 Data strategy and data governance work together to ensure data assets fully support strategy

After many years of helping organizations with data strategy one extremely important realization has floated to the top: If the organizational strategy is not good, a well-articulated data strategy can help harden and reinforce an improved version of the organizational strategy.

A final note: all agree that the data strategy should be the sum of organizational data governance strategy, organizational data quality strategy, organizational metadata strategy, organizational BI/Analytics strategy, organizational data architecture strategy, etc. We prefer the following focused approach as opposed to the massive overplanning that results from attempting to coordinate multiple strategies for relatively immature subdisciplines.

DATA SECURITY COLLABORATION

Supported by research and experience, one position has become very clear. EDEs should be responsible for leveraging organizational data assets and having the same entity be responsible for safeguarding them is a conflict of interest. Instead, EDEs should work with business operations to determine the appropriate data classifications and controls for data while insisting that IT and authorized users follow the rules assigned by business operations. That said, the EDE and data security lead should work closely with one another across the entire data lifecycle, as organizations develop data strategies and data security solutions. Areas of collaboration, for example, include data prioritization and, access. Organizations failing to take advantage of such a relationship risk being disconnected from IT security, having to rework solutions and generally misunderstanding one another.

References

Adams Media (2015). *The Little Book for Dads: Stories, Jokes, Games and More.*

Aiken, P. & Billings, J. (2013). *Monetizing Data Management: Finding the Value in Your Organization's Most Important* Asset. Technics Publications.

Buytendijk, F. & Judah, S. (2015). *A Good Information Management Strategy Starts with Vision and Value*s, 1–10.

Campbell, D. (2002). *Business Strategy.* Routledge.

Carnegie Mellon University. (2014). Data Management Maturity Model v1.0 (pp. 1–248).

Chan, Y. E., Huff, S. L. & Copeland, D. G. (1997). *Assessing realized information systems strategy.* The Journal of Strategic Information Systems, 6(4), 273-298.

Chan, Y. E., Huff, S. L., Barclay, D. W. & Copeland, D. G. (1997). *Business strategic orientation, information systems strategic orientation and strategic alignment.* Information Systems Research, 8(2), 125-150.

Chapman, C. S. (2005). *Controlling Strategy: Management, Accounting and Performance Measurement.* Oxford University Press.

Clarence, J. & Hempfield, W. (2011). *Data Quality? That's IT's Problem Not Mine: What Business Leaders Should Know about Data Quality.* Pittney Bowes Business Insights.

Communications of the ACM, 24(1), 24-33.

Daniell, M. (2006). *Strategy: A Step by Step Approach to the Development and Presentation of World Class Business Strategy* (pp. 1–321).

Daniell, M. (2007). *The Elements of Strategy* (pp. 1–110).

Formisano, R. A. (2004). *Manager's Guide to Strategy*. New York: McGraw-Hill.

Friend, J. & Hickling, A. (2012). *Planning Under Pressure*. Routledge.

Gandellini, G., Pezzi, A. & Venanzi, D. (2013). *Strategy for Action – II*. Milano: Springer Science & Business Media.

Gretzky, W. & Reilly, R. (1990). *Gretzky: An autobiography*. New York, NY: HarperCollins.

Grünig, R. & Kühn, R. (2015). *The Strategy Planning Process*. Berlin, Heidelberg: Springer.

Grünig, R., Clark, A. & Kühn, R. (2010). *Process-Based Strategic Planning*. Berlin, Heidelberg: Springer Science & Business Media.

Harris, H. & Murphy, S. (2013). *Analyzing the Analyzers: An Introspective Survey of Data Scientists and Their Work*. O'Reilly Media.

Hitt, M. A., Ireland, R. D. & Hoskisson, R. E. (2010). *Strategic Management* (pp. 1–843).

Jones, P. (2013). *Communicating Strategy* (pp. 1–199). Gower Publishing Limited.

Keen, P. G. (1981). *Information systems and Organizational Change*.

Kim, W. C. & Mauborgne, R. (2005). *Blue Ocean Strategy* (pp. 1–257). Harvard Business School Press.

Lake Superior State University. (2017). *Lake Superior State University: Banished Words List: 2017*. N.p., n.d. Web. 25 Feb. 2017.

Laney, D., Duncan, A. D., Faria, M., Logan, D., *et al.* (2016). *Predicts 2016: Information Strategy*, 1–12.

Lattin, J.M. & M. Rierson, M. (2007). *Capital One: Leveraging Information-Based Marketing*. [M-316]. Case Studies and Teaching Materials. Stanford University.

Liddell, H, G. & Scott, R. (1999). *A Greek-English Lexicon*, on Perseus.

Lippitt, M. (2003). *Leading Complex Change*. Enterprise Management, LTD.

Lynch, R. (2014). *Strategic Management* (pp. 1–801).

Magretta, J., Porter, M. E. & Magretta, J. P. (1970, January 01). *Understanding Michael Porter: The Essential Guide to Competition and Strategy*.

Marr, B. (2015, July 01). *Where Big Data Projects Fail*. Retrieved from http://bit.ly/2lNV9Ws.

Mintzberg, H. (1978). *Patterns in strategy formation. Management Science*, 24(9), 1–15.

Plotkin, D. (2014). *Data Stewardship*. Elsevier Inc.

Porter, M. E. (1983). *Competitive Strategy*. Simon and Schuster.

Project Management Institute (PMI). (2013). *A Guide to the Project Management Body of Knowledge* (PMBOK® Guide), Fifth Edition.

Robert, J. (2004). *The Modern Firm*. Oxford University Press.

Roberts, A. (2015). *Napoleon: A Life*. N.p.: Penguin. Print.

Rust, J. (July 1985). *Stationary Equilibrium in a Market for Durable Assets. Econometrica* Vol. 53, No. 4, pp. 783-805.

Sports Illustrated. (2012). *The Great One: The Complete Wayne Gretzky Collection*.

Thompson, A., Gamble, J. & Strickland, A. J. III. (2015). *Crafting and Executing Strategy: Concepts and Cases*. McGraw-Hill Higher Education.

Wallace, B. G. (2000). *Patton and His Third Army*. Stackpole Books.

White, C. (2006). *Strategic Management* (pp. 1–877). Palgrave Macmillian.

Wiggins, B. (2012). *Effective Document and Data Management*. Gower Publishing, Ltd.

Williams, K. (2009). *Strategic Management*. DK Publishing (Dorling Kindersley).

Williams, T. (2010). *Positioning for professionals: How professional knowledge firms can differentiate their way to success.* Hoboken, NJ: Wiley.

CHAPTER 2
Data Strategy is Necessary for Effective Data Governance

This chapter begins with a discussion as to why data should not be considered the "new oil," as so many have suggested. It argues against the proposition that big data and data science can solve all data challenges. As you will see, neither concept is sufficiently well-defined to provide sufficient guidance, upon which to base a strategy. Big data technologies are tools and are only one of the necessary elements of P3T. Similarly, data scientists are people and another necessary but insufficient element. While people and tools are critically important, they are incomplete and not integrated. To this end, data strategy—through a governance process—is the force that integrates each P3T element together, making it whole, functional and sustainable. Here are three reasons for creating an organizational data strategy.

1. A data strategy is required to improve an organization's data. It is especially important to understand that data follows Pareto's law that avows 80 percent of organizational data to be redundant, obsolete or trivial (ROT[3]). Improving organizational data involves eliminating data ROT (the clear majority of an

---

[3] Cathy Denton has pointed out that the correct representation should be Redundant Incomplete Obsolete Trivial (RIOT) but this doesn't roll off the tongue as easily so we will stick to ROT.

organization's data) and improving the remaining 20 percent to render it "fit for use."

2. Organizations use data to manage, measure and motivate change. Improving the way all organizational personnel use data—from clerks to data scientists—is necessary because rarely are such individuals trained in the use of data as an organizational asset.

3. Only when the quality of organizational data and data use training for organizational personnel are improved can data assets be optimally employed to support data strategy and organizational strategy.

Managing the unique characteristics of data assets without guidance, that is, a plan, is the least effective thing an organization can do. A data strategy is required to provide input to organizational data governance programs. Failure to do so leaves such programs lacking direction and, thus, failing to fully support organizational strategy.

Increasingly, these strategies depend on organizational data monetizing capabilities. *Facebook* has an estimated value worth more than $200 billion, almost an order of magnitude more than United Airlines (worth $34 billion). What is the difference? Data (La Monica, 2014). Basic data strategy goals are depicted in Figure 2.1 below.

Figure 2.1 Additive data strategy goals

Notice that each goal builds on the previous one: organizations must satisfy each goal to realize full benefits of data. While this may seem restrictive, organizations cannot improve the way staff use data if the data is not yet fit for its intended purpose. Likewise, people cannot make use of data to support strategy if they do not possess the requisite knowledge, skills and abilities (KSA).

An excellent starting point is to agree that a "big bang" implementation (changing everything at once) is impossible for several reasons. The inherent complexity of legacy organizational data environments is a major consideration. Similarly, it would be unproductive to attempt organization-wide instruction for data usage and operational change all at once. So, there's no stretch to recognize the unreasonableness to anticipate success while attempting to align data, people and the strategy simultaneously. Once organizations accept that the plan works incrementally, sequentially and iteratively, the necessity to master the data strategy becomes obvious.

DATA IS *NOT* THE NEW OIL

Google the phrase "data is the new oil", and you will find more than five million references. Clive Humby, a United Kingdom-based researcher, was one of the first to claim that data is the new oil and, just like crude oil, data can be drilled (mined) and refined to provide value (Spijker, 2014). European Commission Vice President Neelie Kroes extended Humby's metaphor, noting that, just as oil had changed entire economies and the way its people lived and worked, data is driving similar kinds of changes today. Its impact can be felt in nearly every part of the global economy from technology, finance and health to retail, manufacturing and research (Spijker, 2014).

While these transformative properties are interesting, this is absolutely the *wrong* way to think about data assets. For instance, oil conforms to a product-use cycle. After one uses it, one must get more oil to obtain additional value, and, when that oil is gone, one must replenish the supply. This process continues until one no longer needs or has oil. Additionally, there is no concept of reuse whatsoever relative to oil. It is finite and predictable and, when it is gone, it is gone. Further, the price of oil fluctuates in response to market forces, unlike data assets that become more valuable with well-managed investments.

Data does not work this way, and applying these same concepts to data makes little sense (Barlow, 2000). In fact, the relative cost of acquiring data is most expensive the first time one uses it. Costs diminish with each subsequent reuse. Therefore, organizations are encouraged and financially rewarded to reuse data.

Instead, organizations keep data in original electronic format, where it will stay unless someone deliberately changes it. Likewise, increased use will not destroy or harm data. In this way, data is durable (capable of generating flows of goods and services over time), and organizations should treat it as an investment rather than an expense. When one compares data to other organizational assets, one quickly sees that data is unique, making it the most powerful yet underutilized and poorly managed organizational asset. Such uniqueness warrants its own strategy.

A better way to conceptualize data is change oil to soil. Plant good things in it and it was produce yield over and over. The timing is better also – one doesn't plant tomato plants on Tuesday and expect to harvest ripe tomatoes on Thursday. It requires preparation and patience.

Figure 2.2 specifies relationships between the terms *data*, *information* and *intelligence*. Intelligence is derived from understanding both information and its associated use. Information, in turn, is derived from data by request. Data is based on facts and meaning.

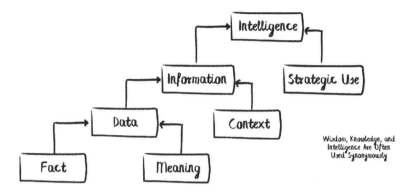

Figure 2.2 A model specifying relationships among closely related terms (Appleton 1986)

1. Each *fact* combines with one or more *meanings*.
2. Each fact and meaning combination is referred to as a *datum*.
3. *Information* is one or more *data* returned in response to a specific *request*.
4. *Information reuse* is enabled when one fact is combined with more than one meaning.
5. *Intelligence* is information associated with its *strategic uses*.

Data assets are stored facts and meanings that are combined to create information. A subset of organizational information is used to assist with achievement of strategic objectives. When combined with requests and put to strategic use, its value increases. (Note: the terms "intelligence," "wisdom," and "knowledge" have all been used interchangeably over the more than 30 years this model has been in use.) Graphically depicting the importance of each architectural layer as a building block used by organizations to leverage data adds elegance to Appleton's (1986) original model.

One cannot build a multistory house on a marshmallow base. If the foundation cannot support higher levels, the entire structure will be crippled. In the same way, each layer of Appleton's model relies on the soundness of both preceding and underlying layer being and ability to support the next higher level. This layered dependency repeats throughout the entire model with each layer supporting the next.

THE POST-BIG DATA ERA

Figure 2.3 is commonly used to define what many imprecisely call "big data."

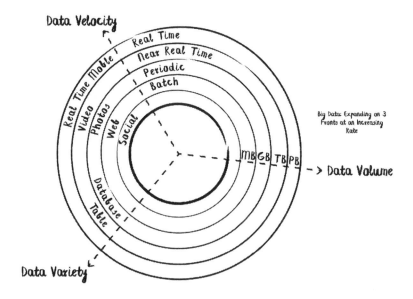

Figure 2.3 Common depiction of big data

During the last decade, it has been popular to write about an ill-defined concept called "big data." The term has always been elusive as there has never been an objective definition. Instead, writers have referred to Doug Laney's observation that the variety, volume and velocity (3 Vs) of data were increasing at a rate faster than then current capabilities were able to process them (Laney, 2001). Writers eager to expand on the alliteration worked their way up to 13 Vs.

VAST	**VERIFIED**	**VERBOSE**	**VISUALIZED**
VOLUME	**VEXINGLY**	**VALUABLE**	**VELOCITY**
VIGOROUSLY	**VARIABLE**	**VITAL**	**VERACITY**

The thirteenth represents **VANITY** of the big data experts (Marshey 1998). Unfortunately, these V-words used to describe the concept of "big data" suffer from terminal vagueness. That is, absent objective measures, the concept of "big data" will always remain in the eye of the beholder. This leads to unfortunate parallels with a famous quote from Supreme Court Justice Potter Stewart.

I shall not today attempt further to define the kinds of material, but I know it when I see it.

One cannot build good science on unusable definitions and an inability to objectively identify big data. Any measurements, claims of success, quantifications must be viewed skeptically. Since big data cannot be objectively identified, it is important to study what can be identified objectively: big data technologies. (All agree that the increase in size mandates engineering approaches.)

BIG DATA TECHNOLOGIES

Readers are urged to experiment. The next time someone wants to have a conversation with you about "big data," ask them instead to talk about "big data technologies." You may be surprised at how different the discussion will be. Gartner removed the term "big data" from its hype cycle in 2015 because its use had become somewhat mainstream. It went so far as to issue a report titled, "The Demise of Big Data, Its Lessons and the State of Things to Come."

By forcing the discussion to explicitly focus on *technologies*, one quickly realizes that *policy, people* and *process* (our P3 of the P3T) need to be addressed. Many think the *people* component as ill-defined as are "big data" and "data scientist." Eric Siegel famously stated that "data science is a redundant term, since all science involves data. It is like saying, "book librarian" (Siegel, 1994). Further, all agree that these specialists spend 80 percent of their time munging data, leaving only 20 percent of their time available for analysis (Harris, 2013). This has led to more creation of hundreds of programs in research, statistics, computer science and many other fields incorporated into data science programs. While this increased scrutiny has been appealing and profitable to participating academic organizations, employers have responded with specific complaints about newly minted data scientists.

- **Skillsets are too generalized.** The term "data scientist" is as vague as "big data." To be useful, the term "data scientist" must be further qualified. Show us an actuarial data scientist, a health data scientist, a chemical data scientist, a weather data scientist, etc., and we can define KSAs required to advance the field (a requisite for any science).

- **They are not interested in learning the business.** As with most technologically-focused careers, this first generation of data scientists has proven more interested in algorithms than in helping organizations use their craft to improve their operations.

- **They are not productive enough.** Eighty percent (80%) of their time is spend migrating, converting and improving data. This ratio can be improved by recognizing the need to both teach more data management principles as part of core data science curricula and partner data scientists with capable and qualified data management professionals at a ratio or 10 data scientists for each data management professional.

In terms of value chain, data scientists are authorized recipients and consumers of organizational data assets. They typically use copies of organizational data to process it into a form by which they can perform various analyses to gather results. Unfortunately, we have yet to see a data science operation that feeds the results of these data munging operations back into production data as lessons learned about data quality, structure or and operations. This represents a further loss to organizational productivity or, as Tom Redman puts it in his latest book, *Getting in Front on Data*: a Hidden Data Factory (2016), requiring the organization to devote unallocated time and effort to correcting data challenges.

Recent advances in data technologies (tools) have resulted in significant new ways of interacting with organizational data assets, despite the vagueness of the promise of "big data." The data science movement has resulted in increased awareness of data skills that organizations are now capitalizing, partially addressing the *people* leg of the triangle. The *process* leg benefits from the data strategy as it provides focus for data governance program initiatives. In other words, big data technologies and industry-specific data scientists can provide organizations some of the resources required to do more with data, but organizations still need a well-defined target and an understanding of their position relative to that gap. The data strategy provides the *what* and organizational data governance provides the *how* for organizations to achieve data goals.

The next three sections will address specific motivations around data strategy development.

MOTIVATION NO. 1: IMPROVING YOUR ORGANIZATION'S DATA

Unfortunately, far too many organizations can make the following statements.

- We do not know what data we have.

- We do not know where all of it is.

- We do not know what people are doing with it.

- We do not know its quality.

- All our data is of unknown quality (a worse version of the previous statement).

Try it privately within your own organization. Ask around about the topic of data; the answers may surprise you. In addition to organizations possessing large amounts of data of unknown quality. This suggests that the best way to improve organizational data assets is to both decrease the organizational ROT and increase the quality of the remaining data.

The value of information in business is rising, and business leaders, more and more, are seeing the ability to govern, manage and harvest information as critical to success (Smallwood, 2014). Raw data is now being increasingly viewed as an asset that can be leveraged, just like financial or human capital. Well–defined, data-related processes will alleviate associated fear, doubt, uncertainty and risk.

There are three primary categories of data value.

DATA POINTS TO THE LOCATIONS OF VALUABLE THINGS

If one were to ask whether you know where your financial investments are, how would you respond? Do you know where your jewelry is? Do you know where your money is? Nearly everyone would respond in the affirmative. Of course, you know where your valuables are. Yet, when it comes to data—something people regularly call their *data assets*, organizations generally have no idea as to:

- which data collections house specific data items (where the data is stored);

- the identity of specific individuals who are using data items to make specific decisions (who is using it and for what);

- the purpose for which the data is collected and accessed; and

- what transformations are being applied to which data collections (what people are doing with specific data collections).

All this falls within the category of metadata management. Improving metadata management capabilities—not just technologies—permits organizations to gain confidence in the amount of data they can process and strategically employ. In today's politically charged climate, not knowing where your data assets are presents unacceptable risk to nearly every organization. Ironically, most organizations lack the P3T infrastructure to effectively and efficiently manage their data assets.

As mentioned, data by itself is valuable. However, data also acts as a reference to where other valuable things might be. In this way, data is the stuff used to help assert and maintain order across the organization. Data, and more specifically metadata, is the information that organizations use to establish and maintain control over all other assets.

DATA HAS INTRINSIC VALUE BY ITSELF

Economists have known for a long time that currency is a proxy for value and that using currency facilitates trade (Hillard, 2010). Today, data is used to record information, typically in the form of discrete transactions. For example, organizations use data to record debits and credits to financial accounts, to reflect the records of automobile repairs and to reserve a seat on an aircraft bound for Tanzania. This is "transactional data." Secondary but important information required or made available for the full or proper use of primary information is referred to as "incidental" or "collateral" data. Above all, however, data today is quickly replacing currency to record the exchange of value such as purchases. At one time organizations used information technology to *save* money for the organization. Today, however, organizations use data to *make* money for the organization. It is becoming apparent that more organizations understand what is happening and are beginning to establish the value of data to the organization.

Theoretically, data could be placed on the company's balance sheet along with other intangible assets like intellectual property, trademarks and order backlogs. In fact, AT&T has done just this. In 2012, it established a value for data, such as customer lists and relationships, at $2.7 billion and put that asset on its balance sheet. In another 2012 SAS study, researchers showed that approximately 20 percent of large companies in the United Kingdom are already assigning financial value to their data and putting those assets on their balance sheets (Van Rijmenam, 2014).

Putting data on a company's balance sheet is not a trivial decision, however, and the process behind doing so should be transparent, objective and repeatable. Instituting a process for accounting for the value of data has other benefits, like having better control over organizational data (Van Rijmenam, 2014). For example, once data has been valued (*i.e.*, monetized), people begin to make better use of it, treating it as a strategic and valuable asset.

However, before organizations begin making rules regarding data and its use, it is critically important to establish an understanding of the value of that data. Despite there being a growing consensus that data *is* an asset, there is still no uniform or common method accepted by various accounting bodies to assert data's value. Additionally, now that there are more knowledge workers using data every day (*e.g.*, actuaries, investors, product researchers and analysts) to make fact-based decisions, we would expect standards to emerge in the not so distant future.

DATA HAS INHERENT COMBINATORIAL VALUE

As has been shown, data by itself has intrinsic or inherent value. However, there is another unique aspect of data: it has a *combinatorial value* when it is intermeshed with other data. For example, Forrester Research (2012) found that the top 15 percent of corporate performers have recognized the combinatorial value of data. These firms now acquire data from other sources and combine it with their data holdings to provide additional insight into their businesses. The number of such firms is growing. In fact, according to the study, more than 30 percent of the respondents use data from external sources. As these companies have seen, the relative value of data explodes when it is combined with other data and, because most data are born digital today, organizations have the opportunity to establish automatic links among data elements during creation. Too many are unaware that data is the input to business processes. Thinking this way will soon help position these organizations for more effective data use (Ohlhorst, 2012).

MOTIVATION NO. 2: IMPROVING THE WAY PEOPLE USE DATA

With so much data, it is easy to see how reducing ROT could improve the way people use organizational data. However, there is an outstanding and foundational obstacle to doing this. People are not prepared to make full use of data assets. Because data is still understood to be a by-product of information technology, people continue to define data in terms of software and systems development. They do not recognize data as being an ongoing process of environmental analysis, choice and adaptation.

Consider this. By the time students are in high school, they have become proficient at using mobile devices. However, they have absolutely no understanding or appreciation for the underlying data and how they should treat it. We, on the other hand, believe that *data education* should be taught in school so that students can begin to learn about data and its value to business success and nearly every aspect of our personal lives. Introducing data education in school would take considerable time to implement, so what is needed now is further education for knowledge workers covering the basics of data awareness. Once people have learned the foundational concepts, organizations should expect to see an increase in efficiencies and productivity and a decrease in overhead cost.

PERCEIVING THE VALUE OF DATA

The world is becoming increasingly connected. Connected people and connected things are creating far-reaching digital networks of interconnected data, and organizations need to learn how to make sense of the proliferation of big and fast data if they are to remain viable in today's competitive environment. It is no longer enough to be successful. Today's organizations are fighting for their very survival. A recent study of senior business leaders showed organizations are quickly implementing big data technologies all around the world (Capgemini, 2015).

In 2015, Capgemini interviewed senior business leaders from more than one thousand companies. They found that more than 61 percent of the respondents acknowledged data was a driver of revenue in its own right and was becoming valuable to their businesses as part of their products and services. One respondent reported that data has the potential to deliver a competitive advantage to any company, and failure to harness it will result in that firm lagging its competitors and risking irrelevancy in the market. To this end, there are three basic ways in which organizations can use data to help better position themselves in the market: (1) measuring changes, (2) managing change, and (3) motivating change.

USING DATA TO MEASURE CHANGE

One way by which organizations are using data is to help them become more efficient and cut costs. Organizations are quickly adapting data analytics to help improve competitive positions and gain efficiencies in the marketplace. Companies around the world continue to improve analytics designed to help cut costs, save time and avoid wasting money with the implementation of scorecards, key performance indicators (KPI), business intelligence and analytics.

An example: news organizations were able to report the 2016 Presidential election results comparing counties in the state of Wisconsin that voted for Barak Obama in 2012 to the number of counties that voted for Hillary Clinton in 2016-illustrating the magnitude of the change in voting.

USING DATA TO MANAGE CHANGE

Many organizations use data to learn new things about their current businesses. In turn, such insights allow them to make informed decisions about what kinds of changes are needed within their existing businesses. For example, some companies are learning new things about their customers' buying behavior, which informs decision-making when adjusting sales and marketing activities.

For some, a much better understanding of customer base is the result of aggregating and analyzing all relevant customers. Other companies acquire data from third party vendors and aggregate it with owned data assets to gain new knowledge about business operations and performance. For example, project management tracks time and resources spent on activities that comprise the critical path. Deviation from forecast time and resources adversely delays overall completion milestones. Reported time and resource expenditures are used to determine future needs required to keep (or put the project back) on track.

Organizational transformation is a well-defined field. It has proven successful in implementing cultural change management. While not addressed here, the reader should consult works such as *Who Moved My Cheese?* by Spencer Johnson (2015) for guidance.

USING DATA TO MOTIVATE CHANGE

Organizations are quickly realizing that success is hinged on an ability to leverage data for their own purposes (see Figure 2.4). An emerging model supports use of data to affect change within the environment in the creation of entirely new lines of business.

A good example of this model is the mapping industry. Where such companies once sold paper maps, they now sell digital mapping products and complementary services. Other sectors are discovering new, data-based offerings as well. The transportation industry has monetized data about passengers and now sells data products to retailers and station locations.

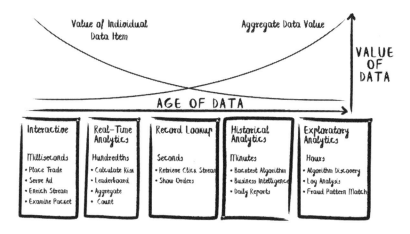

Figure 2.4 Value of data measured over time

Also consider supermarket operator Kroger Co., which records customer purchases at each of its 2,600 stores. The company also tracks the purchasing history of its roughly 55 million loyalty card members (Monga, 2014). Once collected, Kroger sifts through its data looking for trends and, then, through a joint venture, sells the information to vendors who stock Kroger's shelves with goods ranging from cereals to sodas. Consumer product makers, like Procter & Gamble Co. and Nestlé SA. are willing to pay handsomely for those insights as it facilitates tailoring products and marketing to consumer preferences.

Research results reflect that most corporations suffer one major disconnect. Unless and until everyone is more data knowledgeable (i.e., having had better educational grounding about data as an asset), organizations will be unable to better use data to support their strategic initiatives.

MOTIVATION NO. 3: IMPROVING DATA TO SUPPORT ORGANIZATIONAL STRATEGY

In our experiences, employing data assets in support of strategy has proven difficult for most organizations primarily because they attempt to implement change using the wrong mechanism: a project. Implementation of a data strategy must be accomplished at the program level. All organizations that have attempted (and that will attempt) to implement data strategy via a project have failed (and will continue to fail).

Before organizations can leverage data and enjoy its full value, they must first be confident in the quality of their data. To reach this stage, however, organizations must address data management across P3T dimensions, understanding that all areas must mature and that such a pervasive capability can easily take decades to fully master without specific initiatives focused exclusively on these areas.

RESPONDING TO A CHANGING ENVIRONMENT

For organizations to evolve in today's rapidly changing competitive environment, it is essential for them to evolve existing P3T to keep up with such changing environment. As shown in Figure 2.5, most organizations treat data as a by-product, an output or a result of information technology—thus existing somewhere between business and IT.

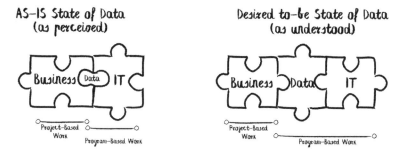

Figure 2.5 Present perception versus desired perception of the role of data organizations

Of note in this figure is the clear change in focus between project- and program-based work. Under present systems, IT is largely project-based with data included as part of the project. Under the desired state, data is included as program-based work and distinct from IT projects.

While it goes without saying that business and IT must collaborate, both groups will need additional training and knowledge as these capabilities do not exist natively. Both must realize that, for information technology and business operations to interoperate smoothly, it is necessary for them to perfectly integrate *at the most granular level*—the data level. At that point, the importance of standardized data becomes obvious. Just as one cannot expect systems to run smoothly with sand in their lubricant, one cannot expect organizations to run smoothly unless the data that connects IT systems to business systems interoperates perfectly.

Today's organizations represent a broad array of businesses: non-governmental and governmental organizations and equities; military and civilian. These businesses cannot succeed without robust and actionable data. Missions are global in nature, reaching nearly every part of the world, and the speed and accuracy with which data can be acquired, processed and exploited are critical capabilities that directly contribute to commercial, civic and national security successes. Because such organizations are diverse in nature, there are many outstanding issues relative to their data and its appropriate use.

Various laws, directives, regulations and policies create confusion as lawmakers push organizations into new and untested legal, cultural and technical territory. As organizations begin to understand how such environmental forces affect them, they will begin to make necessary changes. To this end, these organizations are at an inflection point, one that will likely introduce more change than at any other time in their history. At the heart of this change is data.

Regarding social environments, matters have become even more complex. Organizations are hiring an entirely new generation of employees, one that has a dramatically different perspective on data and its use and handling. For example, mobile computing and web applications are two key computing platforms used by young people every day along with millions of software applications available via online services such as *iTunes*, *Facebook* and *Twitter*. People born after 1990 live their lives in a connected world (Kundra, 2010). They grew up with the Internet, cell phones and social media websites like *YouTube* and *Twitter*, as well as other online services. When these people enter the workforce, they expect the same sort of openness and easy access to data they enjoy outside of work. What they find instead can be an arcane set of data sharing practices, tools and techniques that only serve to confuse and frustrate the new workers. Additionally, as Vivek Kundra noted (2010), young people expect easy access to tools when they are at work.

CREATING A COMPETITIVE ADVANTAGE WITH DATA

Digital technology has changed the competitive landscape and created an increased awareness of a new, less tangible asset: *data*. For the most part, however, organizations are not managing those data assets in any sort of systematic and reproducible manner. Data assets are not managed as other organizational assets, like people, property, money and materials, are managed. Sometimes, data assets are not managed at all. Yet, these same organizations, particularly leadership, expect to derive value from digital assets as with their other assets.

Getting value from data is not a new idea. The idea is as long-standing and well-established as the customer loyalty club, one of the first examples of data monetization. What needs to happen, though, is organizational management of data just like any other corporate asset and building the value of data into return on investment (ROI) calculations.

Once organizations recognize data as something inherently valuable, they can begin taking steps to develop a return on that investment by developing a comprehensive strategic plan. This is often expressed through the organization's mission and vision, including orientation to markets, competition and other environmental factors (Project Management Institute, 2013). An effective strategy also provides direction for development and growth, as well as performance metrics to gauge success. To bridge the gap between organizational strategy and successful business value realization, organizations use a variety of programmatic constructs like portfolios, programs and projects—all of which, by the way, are dependent upon data.

Now more than ever, organizations need to include data management as an element of traditional business activities.

References

Appleton, D. (1986). *Information Asset Management.* Datamation. Newton, MA: Cahners Publishing Company 32, 6.

Barlow, J. P. (2000). *Cybernomics: Toward a Theory of Information Economy.* Retrieved from http://www.ml.com/woml/forum.

Carnegie Mellon University. (2014). *Introduction to DMM Concepts* (pp. 1–118).

Enterprise Data Management Council. (2014). *The Data Management Strategy* (pp. 1–7).

Foresights Strategy Spotlight: *Business Intelligence and Big Data,* Q4 2012.

Harris, H. D. (2013). *Analyzing the Analyzers: An Introspective Survey of Data Scientists and Their Work.*

Hill, K. (2016). *How Target Figured Out a Teen Girl Was Pregnant Before Her Father Did.* Forbes Magazine.

Hillard, R. (2010). *Information-driven business: How to manage data and information for maximum advantage.* John Wiley & Sons.

Hopkins, B. (2013). *The Patterns of Big Data: A Data Management Playbook Toolkit.* Rep. N.p.

Kundra, V. (2010). *25-point implementation plan to reform Federal information technology management (Rep.).* Washington, DC: Office of the Chief Information Officer.

La Monica, P.R. (2014). *A lot to 'like': Facebook now worth $200 billion,* Money.

Laney, D. (2001). *3D data management: Controlling data volume, velocity and variety.* META Group Research Note, 6, 70.

Marshey, J. (1998) Silicon Graphics (widely credited on the internet)

Monga, V. (2014). *The Big Mystery: What's Big Data Really Worth?* The Wall Street Journal.

Ohlhorst, F. & Wiley J. (2012) SAS Business Series: Big Data Analytics: Turning Big Data into Big Money (1). Somerset, US: Wiley, 2012.

Pollock, J. L. (2005). *Thinking About Acting* (pp. 1–266). Oxford University Press.

Project Management Institute (PMI). (2012). *The Standard for Program Management* (pp. 1–187).

Project Management Institute (PMI). (2013). *A Guide to the Project Management Body of Knowledge* (PMBOK® Guide), Fifth Edition.

Redman, T. (2016). *Getting in front on data: Who does what.* Technics Publications.

Runciman, B. & Gordon, K. (2014) *Big Data: Opportunities and challenges.* Swindon, GB: BCS, The Chartered Institute for IT, 2014.

Siegel, E. (2016). *Predictive analytics: The power to predict who will click, buy, lie or die.* Hoboken: Wiley.

Smallwood, R. F. (2014*). Information Governance for Business Documents and Records.* Proceedings of the 39th Annual Hawaii International Conference on System Sciences (HICSS'06) (pp. 464–195b). John Wiley & Sons.

Tittel, E. (2014). *The Dangers of Dark Data and How to Minimize Your Exposure.* CIO. N.p., 24 Sept. 2014. Web.

van Rijmenam, Mark. Think Bigger: Developing a Successful Big Data Strategy for Your Business. Saranac Lake, US: AMACOM, 2014.

Van't Spijker, A. (2014). *The New Oil: Using Innovative Business Models to Turn Data into Profit.* Basking Ridge, NJ: Technics Publications.

CHAPTER 3
Data Strategy Development
Phase I - Prerequisites

Once organizations recognize that data is a strategic asset, they can develop well-defined data requirements for cross-functional IT projects. For organizations to implement these, they must first revise conventional understanding of data and apply that new understanding to programs and projects. Relying on IT projects to change the way organizations make better data sandwiches will not work, period. Instead, change must come from higher levels in the organization where a dedicated data program can ensure that benefits from each IT project are fully leveraged across the enterprise.

DATA BELONGS TO THE BUSINESS

This short section has been adapted from a previous work (Aiken & Billings, 2013). It is critically important to understand that the business is responsible for data ownership before proceeding with any organizational changes. Here are the reasons why.

- IT does not feel the true impact of poor data management practices. Data issues often delay IT projects, causing organizations to pay more for IT than they should.

- Data's impact is greater on business than it is on IT. Organizations are more likely to publicly suffer from data problems while IT is not as likely to suffer.

- IT does not know the business rules that govern data and its use. IT focuses on great technical knowledge but not on understanding how the business uses data in support of decision-making.

- IT does not own or control access to subject matter expertise needed to implement data-centric development practices. IT focuses almost exclusively on how things work, which consumes most of their capacity and leaves little for understanding what the business needs.

- Only the business can competently assign value to data and its use. The business determines whether something is "good enough" or "fit for purpose."

- Because IT specializes in methods, many assume that IT manages data. Data management organizations often report to IT because IT owns methods.

- Most knowledge workers have no idea what methods can be used to develop flexible, adaptable and reusable data.

- CIOs are consumed by technology and technological issues and have no additional capacity.

THREE CRITICAL BARRIERS

Implementing data strategies is not a straightforward exercise and, for many, hard work has not produced noticeable—let alone tangible or valuable—strategic results. Ironically, while organizations have been implementing data strategies for many years, in our combined half century of working in this space, we have observed very few that have successfully managed to produce a data strategy that successfully supports organizational goals.

Three critical barriers must be overcome as organizations attempt to develop and implement an organizational data strategy. Eliminating these is necessary before organizations can reasonably expect to benefit from data strategy efforts.

Organizations successfully implement data strategies using a two-phased approach (see, Figure 3.1). Phase I addresses *Data Strategy Prerequisites*, which are necessary but insufficient to successfully implement Phase II, *Data Strategy Support Iterations* (discussed at length in Chapter 4). The prerequisites are leadership- and structure-focused, representing substantive goals and accomplishments.

The most effective data strategies are those that are institutionalized, visible, actively endorsed by executive management and strengthened by organizational policy. Only when organizations successfully eliminate Phase I obstacles, can they hope to realize benefits in Phase II.

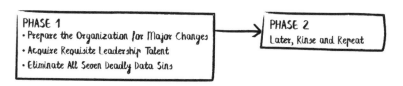

Figure 3.1 Useful data strategies are achieved using a two-phased approach

Phase II determines how data management is defined, organized, funded, governed and integrated into everyday operations within organizations. It further defines the programmatic activities required to employ data in support of organizational strategies. Each iteration becomes a *blueprint* or *plan* describing how organizations will implement mature efforts, harness data and people and ultimately use both of these assets in support of organizational strategy. The remainder of this chapter focuses on the three barriers that prevent most organizations from executing an effective data strategy.

- **Lack of Organizational Readiness.** Organizations need to realize the need for a formal method to change how the organization thinks about data. Without this, the organization will not have the executive endorsement that it needs to institutionalize a data program. (**Note:** The term, "program," as used throughout, refers to *program management*, not software programs.)

- **Unrecognized Lack of Qualified Talent.** If organizations fail to recognize the lack of qualified talent, they will not be able to attract the right people to help them successfully implement data strategies.

- **Failure to Address the Seven Deadly Data Sins.** New talent must be ready to eliminate the Seven Deadly Data Sins before proceeding to Phase II. These sins prevent organizations from succeeding with data.

BARRIER NO. 1: LACKING ORGANIZATIONAL READINESS

Most organizations do not consider organizational readiness when trying to develop a data strategy. Organizations need to define, adopt and implement the P3T component prerequisites of a data strategy. Failing to adequately prepare the organization creates a mismatch between what organizations *can* do and what they *want* to do. You have probably heard the expression: a fool with a tool is still a fool. This idea is equally expressive as follows.

Just because an organization has a method or tool does not guarantee that the method or tool will work for that organization; likewise, if an organization uses a method or tool, it will likely have few, if any, positive effects.

The actions required for organizations to improve data assets, the ways in which personnel use that data and the ways organizations use data to support strategy require fundamental, organization-level changes that must be formally implemented and managed. These changes include:

- structural shifts in the responsibilities of some key executives;

- recognizing most organizations cannot competently interview candidates;

- fundamental changes in the way organizations implement and coordinate important IT and business initiatives; and

- implementing a disciplined approach to data strategy, its sequence and its dependencies.

Mario Faria of Gartner has written of the required changes when preparing to implement them. His list includes other insightful factors:

- cultural resistance to change;

- lack of understanding of the role of data leadership;

- lack of stakeholder involvement and support;

- lack of resources and funding to support the programs; and

- lack of focus in defining the most important initiatives.

These required changes often trigger a range of reactions across the organizations: confusion, uncertainty, doubt, resentment and resistance (Faria et al, 2016). Generally, these changes will require major organizational change initiatives guided by knowledgeable leadership and implemented by competent change management professionals. Failure to prepare for, support and sustain these changes, however, ensures organizations will fail as they attempt subsequent Phase II activities.

BARRIER NO. 2: FAILING TO COMPENSATE FOR LACK OF DATA KNOWLEDGE

This barrier addresses the lack of talent and lack of qualified personnel to interview and hire this talent, an unwillingness to implement required organizational change and accepting the fact that you will not usually find all the requisite knowledge, skills and abilities in a single individual.

LACKING QUALIFIED LEADERSHIP TALENT

Most organizations do not have data-literate personnel who can make informed decisions regarding data in decision making roles. There is a lack of qualified leadership in large part because there are few educational programs at colleges and universities addressing data management. Lacking foundational education leads to a conundrum: if individuals do not possess the requisite data KSAs, how will organizations know whom to hire to help them get smarter about data? Lacking foundational KSAs hurts organizational decision-making in these and other areas across the organization and engenders negative results.

- Non-information technology (IT) students learn virtually nothing about how to manage data. They reinvent and/or discover well-established practices on a project-by-project basis via on-the-job training. This represents a huge source of untapped productivity— from an individual project basis as well as from greater contribution to the research community. Increasingly, prestigious journals and grant-funding institutions require more stringent levels of data asset sharing, transparency and availability.

- IT students typically take one course that is focused on development of a new, physical database, learning in the process that data management is a technical skill required for the development of new databases. Unfortunately, this approach has reinforced the belief that data management is a technical discipline, rather than a logical, strategic business discipline and it is not worthy of management attention (Aiken et al, 2011).

- A study by the international professional organization for data managers, Data Management Association (DAMA.org), reveals that most seek out data management as a profession after 10 years in IT, frustrated that more is not done to support data management (Perez, 2006). When combined with results showing the vast scope of CIO responsibilities, it is no wonder the number of self-rated successful data management practices has fallen from more than 43 percent in 1981 to less than 15 percent in 2007 (*ibid.*).

HIRING PANELS ARE NOT QUALIFIED TO HELP

Without the necessary education, organizations will continue to work and hire people as they always have, which, as we have shown, does not serve the organization's strategic needs. Compounding this problem, many EDEs have not realized they do not know much about managing organizational data assets; consequently, they are not prepared to lead data management activities. Most of the well-meaning individuals who sit on hiring panels do not know enough about data. Likewise, most hiring panels are unqualified to recruit, evaluate and compensate data leadership positions.

Due to their lack of basic understanding, it is unlikely that organizations will be able to identify and hire the right person to be their first data executive. Sadly, once organizations recognize that they hired the wrong person, the entire recruitment process begins unimproved. Hiring unqualified candidates negatively affects the organization and its ability to satisfy its organizational strategy, much less develop a successful data strategy. Consultants, hiring-pools and experienced CDOs/EDEs can be used to offset these deficiencies, but that comes at cost.

Figure 3.2 Crafting change is hard, but implementing change is even harder (DILBERT © 2012 Scott Adams)

CHANGING CAN BE HARD

Saying change can be hard does not make change any easier, and refusing to acknowledge that changing is hard makes changing even harder. (See Figure 3.2) Saying it another way: most data strategies cannot work because there is organizational inertia and dysfunction embedded within and amongst critical operational factors. To create an organizational climate that is ready to leverage data as a strategic asset, the organization must make fundamental but healthy changes.

Fortunately, the field of change management is well-researched, and there are excellent models for organizations to follow. For example, we have often used Mary Lippitt's diagnostic tool, Managing Complex Change, since its original publication in 1987 (Lippitt, 2003). See Figure 3.3.

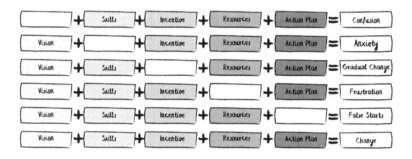

Figure 3.3 Managing complex change (adapted from Lippitt, 1987)

In addition to applicants having a fundamental understanding of change management, applicants need to have a basic understanding of data and data management practices to effectively direct an enterprise program. Over the years, we have met only a handful of people with these skills and abilities, and finding them all in a single individual is nothing short of a daunting and perhaps impossible task. However, these individuals do exist. Sometimes they are easier to find inside your organization, so look there before you look outside your organization.

THERE ARE NO UNICORNS

While it may seem odd, the first EDE is needed to essentially break some eggs and correct some of the longstanding issues related to how organizations have treated data assets. Doing this prepares the way for subsequent executives who can affect real and long-lasting change across the organization. For the first data executive, though, the individual must be thick-skinned, an innovative thinker, have excellent communication skills and possess entrepreneurial knowledge, skills and abilities.

Further, individuals wanting to succeed with data are more often concerned with data-focused KSAs than with "soft" skills. Consequently, locating individuals with these interests, much less individuals who are aware of the need for these KSAs, has been difficult.

THE FIRST EDE IS OFTEN UNSUCCESSFUL

We believe there are no unicorns, no magic potions and no easy solutions to this problem, and we know change is immensely difficult. What this means in practical terms is the first EDE hired will likely incur the wrath of an organization deeply rooted in culture, tradition and parochial behaviors. Each of these forces serves as an impediment to change. To position the organization for success and align its data strategy to the overall organizational strategy, the first EDE must make the most wrenching changes, rapidly. This has presented a fatal risk to the careers of some of our colleagues. To date, many have failed the first attempt. As a result, the second EDE often gets credit for the work of the first.

BARRIER NO. 3: ELIMINATING THE SEVEN BARRIERS TO LEVERAGING DATA

There are seven barriers that organizations need to eliminate before they can successfully implement truly effective data strategies and leverage their data. Known as the *Seven Deadly Data Sins*, most organizations have chosen not to explicitly confront these forces. Figure 3.4 depicts the deadly data sins.

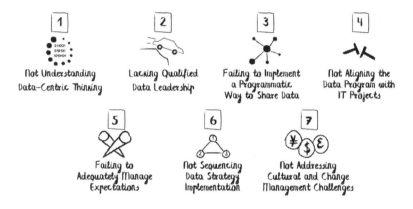

Figure 3.4 Seven Deadly Data Sins

Organizations with a willingness to change and the requisite talent still cannot implement a data strategy unless the organization:

1. understands the underpinnings of data-centric thinking;

2. obtains qualified leadership for data initiatives;

3. separates data and software development;

4. sequences IT projects and the data program properly;

5. manages expectations;

6. sequences its data strategy appropriately; and

7. addresses cultural and change management aspects of data programs.

The capabilities expressed in these sins constitute the foundation upon which data projects, initiatives, technologies and strategies are built. Because the foundation—the sum of these capabilities—is only as strong as its weakest component, it is imperative for organizations to overcome these barriers as early as possible. Failure to eliminate all of them will prevent organizations from successfully implementing a data strategy. Each is described below. Note: This process begins a longer set of evolutionary steps toward managing enterprise data as a strategic asset.

DATA SIN NO. 1: FAILING TO UNDERSTAND DATA-CENTRIC THINKING

The ideas and motives at the foundation of data-centric thinking require that certain topics become cornerstones of a required academic data curriculum. Currently, most colleges and universities do not consider these concepts as base or core concepts. Most are not taught at all, and it will likely take decades to successfully introduce these ideas into traditional academic thinking. When learning institutions ultimately do accept and incorporate these ideas into curricula, they will begin to advance knowledgeable data professionals. Until then, however, organizations will have to rely on professional organizations, like the Data Management Association (DAMA) International, the Association for Federal Information Resource Management (AFFIRM), the International Association for Information and Data Quality (IAIDQ), the Capability Maturity Model Integration (CMMI) Institute (*Capability Maturity Model Integration Data Management Maturity (CMMI/DMM*SM)), the International Society of Chief

Data Officers (ISCDO) and others to fill this knowledge gap and increase the maturity of data practitioners.

Like other fields of study, data management requires a solid, considerate and comprehensive educational foundation. Just as you cannot build any structure on a poorly designed foundation, organizations need solid foundational data management practices if they are to effectively and efficiently leverage data. For example, organizations need to standardize the way they acquire, process, store, and share data assets. Without these core services and capabilities, organizations at every level will continue to invent their own ways of doing things to the detriment of the enterprise. It is incumbent on every organization and its leadership to ensure that all participants—not just the data management team—increase the organization's data literacy and understand these principles to successfully leverage data. This is not an easy task because few in leadership circles understand the foundational underpinnings of data management. Leaders who do not know what they truly need to know, put the organization in a delicate and precarious situation. Until academia develops a data curriculum, organizations will bear the cost of poor data literacy.

Compounding matters, organizational leadership does not realize that data management work is grounded in architecture and engineering, and it cannot easily be combined with software development or other information technology project-based work. When organizations try otherwise, two very costly things happen: (1) data management is treated as a part of individual projects and (2) business expects IT to do it correctly. What should be done instead? Data management professionals collaborate with businesses to abstract their needs into actionable data requirements for the enterprise.

In the end, the point is really quite simple: organizations cannot implement a data strategy without first becoming more knowledgeable and developing the appropriate KSAs required to transform the organization from an IT focus to a data focus. There is no shortcut, no quick-win for developing these capabilities. Organizations need to invest time, money and resources to develop a foundational capability that will ultimately mature into a sustainable enterprise set of services. At the same time, organizations need to carefully level-set expectations by communicating the fact that capabilities will mature over years, sometimes over decades. Importantly, we cannot currently rely on the educational system to supply foundational knowledge about this important field, and this deficiency will take years to correct.

DATA SIN NO. 2: LACKING QUALIFIED DATA LEADERSHIP

For nearly every executive position today, there is at least one educational path for students to follow. For instance, if someone were interested in becoming a chief executive officer, numerous degree programs that claim to prepare the student for the challenges of running a company. The most obvious example is a graduate degree in business administration, more commonly known as a Master of Business Administration (MBA). Likewise, if someone were interested in becoming a chief financial officer, schools offer numerous degree programs to support this need. However, if someone were interested in becoming an EDE, one would discover that, outside of one specific program at UALR,[4] colleges and universities offer few specific or holistic programs of study. Instead, some schools offer selected topics scattered across many different programs,

---

[4] http://ualr.edu/chiefdataofficers

most notably within the library and information science and business programs.

Because our educational system treats data as part of a technical discipline, the knowledge base needed to manage large, complex issues and activities associated with data simply does not exist within our academic institutions. So, while organizations are rapidly realizing a need for someone who is exclusively focused on data, there is not much of viable candidate pool. In many instances, organizations basically appoint someone they believe to most closely represent their needs and generally default to information technology experts. This means the newly-appointed data leader tends to view data issues as technical challenges requiring technical solutions. Lacking qualified data leadership prevents organizations from finding and securing qualified leaders who are well-versed in data. Because the EDE role is still new and lacking an academic and credentialed foundation, organizations are largely unaware of the business process, architecture and engineering requirements needed to successfully reuse and optimize data assets.

Sadly, today, data management embodies only a few scientific, research, architectural or engineering principles, which largely consist of a collection of relatively new and immature industry standards and courses sprinkled across various academic programs. Thus, finding organized data management knowledge is difficult to do, and little of this knowledge exists in most organizations. Except for the DAMA *Data Management Body of Knowledge* (DMBOK) and Carnegie Mellon's *Data Management Maturity Model*, there is virtually no vendor-agnostic data management reference material available. Consequently, organizations must look to professional organizations and qualified consultants to fill the gap.

One can see strong similarities with the introduction and acceptance of the chief financial officer (CFO) role. The CFO is primarily responsible for managing the financial assets of an organization. This officer is also responsible for financial planning and record-keeping, as well as financial reporting to higher management. In some sectors, the CFO is also responsible for analysis of data. Most CFOs of large organizations have finance qualifications such as a Master of Business Administration (MBA) or a Master of Science (MS), or they come from an accounting background. They may also have certifications such as Certified Public Accountant (CPA), Chartered Accountant (CA), Certified Management Accountant (CMA), Chartered Certified Accountant (CCA) or an equivalent status, such as master of finance. When the role of CFO was first introduced, such competencies and credentials did not exist.

Today's CFO is singularly focused on financial matters. This person possesses the requisite KSAs to handle a wide range of financial matters from investment and acquisition to payroll and accounting. Moreover, CFOs have become an expected role within nearly every organization, and CFOs typically occupy their positions for more than a decade for each job or assignment (WEBCPA Staff, 2010). The academic curriculum, training and certifications are mature, and well-established. Organizations can be confident there is a large, qualified candidate pool when they need a CFO. Additionally, CFOs need a broad range of skills beyond the skills needed in accounting. For example, they must first be a business strategist and comfortable with technology. Built on this, CFOs develop financial strategies to increase organizational growth and profitability and create plans and opportunities to optimize the organization's financial assets.

However, if data is truly an asset, one would expect to see similar education and credentials for EDEs, but we do not. Instead, one quickly learns that there are no formalized leadership qualifications, and there is no consensus as to what kinds of certifications are appropriate for the new EDE. Because there is no generally accepted set of educational and data management credentials, it is not surprising many organizations have trouble identifying the right person to lead the organization's data management work. Further, because there is no accepted data management educational regime, finding the right person is problematic, expensive and frustrating to many organizations. Unless and until organizations realize optimizing the full value of its data requires a singularly focused, qualified and responsible individual, organizations will not be able to change current thinking. We need to influence the academic community to develop and offer a rigorous curriculum dedicated to training data professionals.

DATA SIN NO. 3: FAILING TO IMPLEMENT A PROGRAMMATIC WAY TO SHARE DATA

People often ask how data fits into IT projects. *This is the wrong question to ask.* In a nutshell, organizations need to recognize that data requirements evolve at a rate, cadence, rhythm and speed that are fundamentally different from those associated with IT projects. So, the first question to be addressed by an organization is: how should data be incorporated into a portfolio of IT projects?

Figure 3.5 illustrates the relationship between IT projects and the development of shared organizational data. The figure shows that IT operates per a standardized and repeatable project-based method to control production costs and improve delivery performance. Data, however, is different-evolving, as opposed to project-focused. Shared data must be developed, documented and managed separately from, external to and prior to all IT projects. This work is foundational as data must be defined and stored once before it can be used and—more importantly—reused on any individual project. It does not happen accidentally; neither does it happen absent a data strategy. Making this kind of change requires a deliberate and controlled effort across organizations.

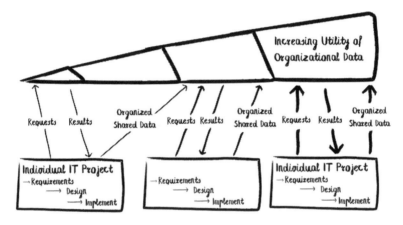

Figure 3.5 Individual IT projects make increasing use of an organizations shared data

The real question, *where* do IT projects fit into data management activities, is the first for organizations to answer. For example, IT projects exist for a fixed period to provide specific solutions to very particular recordkeeping and analytical needs. Underlying these problems is the notion that data exists beyond any project, and that data continues to evolve for as long as the organization exists. Additionally, it is important to note that data evolves at a slower, steadier pace different from technology. For example, an organization may pursue a business goal to enter a new market. The data the organization needs to achieve that goal may precede any IT project by months or even years. After the company enters the market, employees may use IT solutions to help automate certain business processes and functions. Meanwhile, the business may realize it needs other data to bolster its market position, fend off competitors or introduce new products and services.

Even though data requirements evolve outside any particular IT project, organizations need to recognize there are appropriate times to bridge these two activities in a predictable and controlled manner. What typically happens, however, is that organizations task specific IT projects to identify the data needed by the organization. When this happens, projects address their needs at the expense of the enterprise needs.

Operating this way presents an interesting problem. Projects, by definition, operate according to a finite amount of time. They have discrete beginnings, middles and ends. Consequently, it would be wrong to assume a narrowly-focused, finitely-timed effort would be able to quickly, accurately and completely identify the information needed by the entire enterprise to successfully operate. Additionally, it would be wrong to presuppose these same IT projects would have the capability to develop the business processes and rules that would allow the organization to share its data in an unambiguous, predictable and accountable manner.

What does make sense, though, is that this kind of work needs to be performed on a continual basis. Were this the case, data analytical work could provide distinct input to any IT project, thereby reducing the amount of work individual projects would need to accomplish. Working in this manner also increases the likelihood of developing solutions with data specifications that are thoroughly vetted and approved at the enterprise level. The main idea is that data, its requirements, its suitability, its form and its semantics continue to evolve as the business responds to environmental changes. In other words, organizational requirements do not stop when an IT project is complete.

It is important to note that IT projects contain important motivational distinctions that sometimes work in opposition to the development of shared organizational data. Data management does not fit the IT project paradigm because data must precede any IT project definition. Putting it another way, the development of an organization's data assets must occur prior to implementing a specific IT project. Additionally, organizations need to realize it will take considerable time, maybe even years, to evolve current practices from how they work today to the way organizations need them to work. Leadership, in turn, must understand how both systems work to achieve the right balance within the organization.

A good example of this is how organizational data needs are managed. Organizations need to develop ways to better respond to changing organizational data requirements and improved understanding of existing data requirements independent of any IT project. Put simply, to leverage organizational data assets, organizations need to focus effort on understanding true data needs without the distractions associated with IT projects. Without this abstraction, it is impossible to accurately specify data requirements for any IT project. What needs to happen instead is that enterprise data requirements need to evolve separately from, external to and ahead of individual IT projects. This concept is deceptively simple and direct, yet it is probably the most difficult data sin to overcome as so many organizations are disproportionately focused on IT and hoping that IT will give them a competitive advantage.

DATA SIN NO. 4: FAILING TO COORDINATE THE DATA PROGRAM WITH IT PROJECTS

Asking data initiatives to report to IT project management creates an unsolvable and intractable conflict. IT projects are just that: projects. They have discrete beginnings, middle, and ends. However, as we have shown, organizational data must be researched, reviewed, designed and engineered at a level above individual IT projects. IT projects are designed to deliver IT solutions. Understanding what data the enterprise needs to establish or maintain a competitive position is a completely different undertaking and should be managed by an executive with a business background who is charged with managing the organization's data assets. This is no different than what other executives do today. In other areas, executives are charged with managing other kinds of organizational assets like finances, property and personnel, and they perform this work in an ongoing and uninterrupted manner. Those executives may spawn specific projects to accomplish things, but the overall work is a capital endeavor and continues without interruption for the life of the organization. Importantly, IT should not be able to do anything with data without business approval.

The kind of work data executives perform is a *program*. Work is initiated and continues until the organization decides it no longer needs to perform this kind of work (Project Management Institute, 2001). Along the way, the organization can sponsor multiple programs, projects and specific activities that constitute the overall data program.

The confusion surrounding *data jurisdiction* creates other, more expensive and time-consuming problems. For example, when one looks for a root cause of poor quality data, one quickly realizes there is a fundamental misperception about who really owns the problem. When asked, survey after survey of business professionals indicate they think data quality is performed by

IT, who in turn think data quality is a function performed by the business (Aiken & Billings 2013, Aiken & Gillenson *et. al.*, 2011 and Eckerson, 2001). Over the last 30 years, industry has conditioned people to believe data is an IT problem and that the CIO is responsible for solving it. However, CIOs must consider many things other than data, and data quality has fallen into the crack between business and IT (Hempfield, 2011). Research has shown that only approximately 10 percent of all organizations achieve a positive return on investments in data management, while about 30 percent achieve negative ROI results (Aiken et al, 2011).

Hopefully it is becoming clear that organizations should be managing data assets in a way that is dramatically different from what is currently done. Organizations need to create a new position within the business side of the organization, the appropriate home for the EDE. Once understood, common organizational data needs can be maintained within the business side of the organization, and data management would be able to provide well-defined data and data requirements to individual IT projects.

In time, individual IT projects would be able to use data, metadata and data engineering artifacts to help them at the onset of IT work. Having data standards and specifications available to each IT project would reduce the amount of work and confusion IT projects regularly encounter. Instead, IT projects would be able to incorporate well-known, well-understood data plans into each IT project plan, thereby increasing the volume, scope and utility of information given to developers.

When new processes are matured, each new IT system would—by using metadata—be able to provide highly descriptive feedback to data management experts. For organizations to do so, however, they must first revise their understanding of data and apply that new understanding to projects and programs. Simply directing IT workers to change the way they operate will not work. Instead, this change must come from higher levels in the organization where a dedicated data management component can ensure the benefits from each specific IT project are leveraged across the enterprise. Often, this can only be accomplished by an organizational mandate. There are, however, certain parts of data management that are responsibilities shared with IT. Figure 3.6 illustrates this concept using the DAMA's DMBOK.

Figure 3.6 The *Data Management Association's Body of Knowledge* (DAMA DMBOK) shows which functions should be the responsibility of data management

This model presents 10 knowledge areas. Using the DAMA model, data governance, data architecture management, data quality management, document and content management, data warehousing and business intelligence management, metadata management, data security management, and, reference and master data management (MDM) are activities that would report to the EDE. Data development and database operations management are activities that would report to the CIO as they are largely technology functions.

To put these ideas into context, comparing data-centric thinking to traditional IT project development practices illustrates the predicament in which data management professionals find themselves. Figure 3.7 shows the traditional IT project development practices that most organizations follow today. This figure shows where data and information typically fall within IT's planning activities. Generally, considering data is the last activity performed after the organization creates new or identifies existing IT projects.

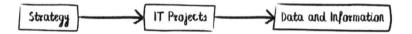

Figure 3.7 Traditional IT project development practices are application-centric

Using this approach, organizations produce their overall organizational strategy. The organization then defines specific IT projects that presumably help satisfy that strategy. At the end of this, individual IT projects determine what data and information the organization uses to be competitive. Clearly, there are issues with this approach—it is misaligned. Business operations determine what data is needed, yet the opposite typically occurs. For example, business processes and data are tightly integrated in software applications, making them difficult to maintain, change and evolve. Working under this model also means very little data can be reused with an IT-focused approach, and data requirements are focused around software applications instead of the organization. Figure 3.8 shows a fundamental shift in thinking to a data-centric set of practices.

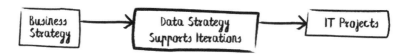

Figure 3.8 Data-centric strategy implementation

As before, organizations define their overall business strategies. Next, data management specifies the data initiatives required to achieve strategic goals and objectives, with an eye toward organization-wide usage and derived from a shared, useful data architecture. Once done, IT projects receive definitions, specifications and other programmatic artifacts at the onset of their work. Working this way, IT is not solely responsible for performing enterprise-level analysis. Instead, IT can focus on technical solutions, which have already been aligned and normalized with an organization's data needs. Additionally, organizations would be able to specify IT projects using the smallest possible footprint and simplest design because they would be leveraging an existing organizational data model. This is also illustrated in Figure 3.9.

This approach offers many distinct advantages over the traditional IT approach. For instance, data assets can be developed in a true enterprise manner. IT projects would subsequently support organization-wide data needs, and the work would complement and automate various business processes. Additionally, organizations could maximize data sharing and reuse as well as reducing brittleness associated with combining data and software. Taken together, this approach increases data sharing, reduces data duplication and waste and improves maintenance, particularly in cases where data is shared across functional areas.

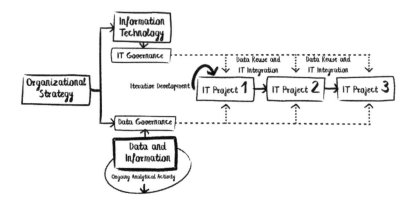

Figure 3.9 Data-centric thinking and development practices

This approach increases data and metadata reuse and provides clearer and better understood business and technical requirements. This approach also produces more productive knowledge workers and better integration with evolving business processes and practices. In the end, it becomes clear: implementing a data-centric approach can produce fewer, less complicated, higher quality and easier-to-maintain software and information technology systems, while leveraging data for strategic organizational initiatives.

DATA SIN NO. 5: FAILING TO ADEQUATELY MANAGE EXPECTATIONS

Before organizations can take advantage of this approach, they must first do two things: (1) manage expectations and (2) align organizations to the new paradigm. It is important to note both activities are prerequisites to taking advantage of the data-centric model.

Achieving tangible behavioral changes can take years to root and mature. It is incumbent on the EDE to ensure the organization understands how data management directly and positively affects the organization's ability to satisfy the goals and objectives of its strategy.

Led by the EDE, the organization needs to develop corporate data management competencies in a series of chartered data management programs, projects and activities. Along the way, the EDE must set and manage organizational expectations. This means carefully balancing the changes that need to occur with delivering real-world, tangible and measurable results. Too much of one or the other will be unsustainable over the long term.

While it can be extremely challenging to show how data supports the organization's strategy, it is equally challenging to manage expectations for new data management initiatives. If organizations want to use data as a resource, they first must understand its dualistic nature—organizations will either leverage data in support of their organizational strategies or that same data will be an impediment. There is no neutral position, and organizations need to control the forces that would otherwise prevent them from taking full advantage of their data resources.

Organizational leaders need to recognize and respect that making these kinds of changes will take time. The EDE needs to clearly articulate an agenda that is balanced between developing specific capabilities and measurable outcomes and the need to describe the agenda in a way that allows others to assign value to the overall initiative. As long as organizations maintain an IT-centric approach to their work, EDEs will have to explain why data architecture—and data management, in general—requires time to do it and do it well. Also, these executives will have to defend the results of data architecture work—until a proven ROI can be established.

While organizations long to exploit big data and perform advanced analytics, organizations need to realize they must first crawl, then walk, then run relative to their data. If organizations truly want to trust the results of their computational abilities, they must be able to account for their data across the entire data lifecycle, from acquisition through final disposition.

The only way to accomplish this is for data management and IT experts to work together as a team. As their KSAs mature, they must capture that new knowledge to guide those who follow. Consider the adage: How does one get to Carnegie Hall? Answer: Practice. Practice. Practice. Organizations also need to realize they cannot simply go out and buy these capabilities, as tempting as this may be. Led by the EDE, these capabilities need to be organic and sustainable over time. Only by understanding existing organizational capabilities, strengths and weaknesses can they hope to achieve mastery in this area.

DATA SIN NO. 6: FAILING TO SEQUENCE DATA STRATEGY IMPLEMENTATION

William Porter's book (1980), *Understanding How to Successfully Implement Data-Based Strategies*, highlighted the need to make fundamental strategic choices between innovation and improved operations. Porter suggested organizations need to understand that most data management teams cannot be innovative, efficient and effective all at once. Instead, they must practice their tradecraft, realize tangible value and leverage their knowledge for future use. Not surprisingly, this explains why today's *big data* projects succeed at rates comparable to IT projects (Marr, 2015) and why the recent expectations of investments in data science have produced less than stellar results (Harris & Murphy, 2013).

What should be happening, instead, is the sequencing and synchronization of the data strategy with IT projects. In practical terms, this means organizational data management practices and associated maturity generally follow a progression through the four quadrants shown in Figure 3.10.

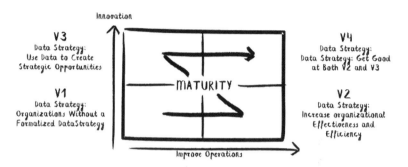

Figure 3.10 Sequencing organizational data *foci*

For organizations at V1, data is not seen as being strategically important to the organizational strategy, and organizations do little with data management that transcends individual work group levels beyond "keeping the doors open." Moreover, the organization does not manage its data, nor does it understand data as a strategic asset. What the organization does, instead, is expend minimal effort toward maintaining data to sustain its operations. The organization focuses its effort on reporting cash-balances instead of developing cash-forecasting abilities.

Organizations that exist at V2 follow a data strategy that is focused primarily on increasing organizational effectiveness and efficiencies, which could be applicable for supporting lean supply chain or low-cost provider models. Organizations that exist in V3 have realized data can help them reinvent themselves and help them establish better positions within the market. A good example of this is Capital One, which is an often-cited example of innovation and modernizing in the arena of providing products for underserved credit populations

(Lattin & Rierson, 2007). However, organizations that recognize the value of data and use it in support of their strategic plans often do so at great expense and often have less than stellar returns on their investments. Those that are in V4 are organizations that have mastered data management practices in V2 and V3. It is important to realize most organizations require a complete reset with respect to this sin. New EDEs must use their organization's data strategy to secure long-term investments, including specific capital investments in training and education and—then and only then—in selected technologies.

DATA SIN NO. 7: FAILING TO ADDRESS CHANGE MANAGEMENT CHALLENGES

For organizations to leverage data as a strategic asset, organizations must mature their technical abilities using change management processes that most do not have. This kind of work is well known, however, and organizations can proceed with the necessary changes with relatively low risk levels (Keen, 1981). The key thing to remember when beginning this work is to stay focused on separating data management from IT management. If organizations do not stay focused on maintaining this separation, they will likely end up like many other quality management initiatives: failing and being labeled as just another management fad. Per management guru Peter Drucker (2006), "Culture eats strategy for breakfast." For organizations to successfully implement the kind of changes that will help them use data as a strategic asset, they must make fundamental changes in both information technology and business. Such changes will be global and affect nearly every part of the organization, but these changes will also be instrumental in securing executive sponsorship, generating momentum and realizing the business vision.

To provide a simple example of this phenomenon, consider the following. Leadership is charged with eliminating the Seven Deadly Data Sins, but the requisite KSAs required to even attract, let alone hire and retain, enterprise data leadership are missing. So, even though the organization has identified a way to get past problem of lacking qualified data management leadership, the organization and the EDE need to address and resolve the Seven Deadly Data Sins before they try to develop smooth-running versions for their data strategy process. When organizations believe that they have completed Phase I activities, they need to stop, take stock of their work and objectively measure performance. They need to be sure they have eliminated the Seven Deadly Data Sins before continuing to Phase II.

What happens often, however, is that individuals will begin to aggressively pursue their own versions of Phase II, not realizing they have not satisfied Phase I prerequisites. When this happens, organizations begin investing significant corporate capital and accomplishing little in terms of lasting change. This accounts for the vast number of EDE failures to date. In such cases, we have recommended the hiring of someone outside the organization. This person will be a "sacrificial lamb" of sorts and be the individual who endures the organizational backlash to the necessary Phase I changes. Once Phase I is complete, the first EDE would help hire a replacement, and the second EDE would proceed to the Phase II tasks.

References

Aiken, P., & Billings, J. (2013). Monetizing Data Management: Finding the Value in Your Organization's Most Important Asset. Technics Publications.

Aiken, P., Gillenson, M., Zhang, X., Raffner, D., "Data Management and Data Administration: Assessing 25 Years of Practice" *Journal of Database Management* 22(3):24-44 July-September 2011.

Chan, Y. E., Huff, S. L., & Copeland, D. G. (1997). Assessing realized information systems strategy. The Journal of Strategic Information Systems, 6(4), 273-298.

Chan, Y. E., Huff, S. L., Barclay, D. W., & Copeland, D. G. (1997). Business strategic orientation, information systems strategic orientation and strategic alignment. Information systems research, 8(2), 125-150.

DILBERT © 2012 Scott Adams. Used by permission of ANDREWS MCMEEL SYNDICATION. All rights reserved.

Faria, M., Logan, V. A., & Popkin, J. (2016). *How to Overcome Critical Roadblocks to Succeed as Chief Data Officer*, 1–7. Retrieved from http://gtnr.it/2mxeeuH.

Harris, H., Murphy, S., & Vaisman, M. (2013). *Analyzing the Analyzers: An Introspective Survey of Data Scientists and Their Work*. O'Reilly Media, Inc.

Hempfield, C. W., Jr. (2011). *Data Quality? That's IT's Problem Not Mine: What Business Leaders Should Know About Data Quality*.

Project Management Institute (PMI). (2001). *A Guide to the Project Management Body of Knowledge* (PMBOK® Guide).

CHAPTER 4
Data Strategy Development
Phase II - Iteration

Organizations have prepared for dramatic change and determined how to do the work. They have also recruited qualified EDEs to oversee the transformation and behavioral changes, and they have eliminated the Seven Deadly Data Sins. Now let us focus on the practical matter of producing a data strategy, some of the obstacles that confront this work, what organizations should consider when they produce their data strategies and what they should include in their documentation. In this chapter, we describe the specific steps involved in developing, implementing and communicating a data strategy. This work is part of Phase II, and we assume organizations have already completed the Phase I prerequisites.

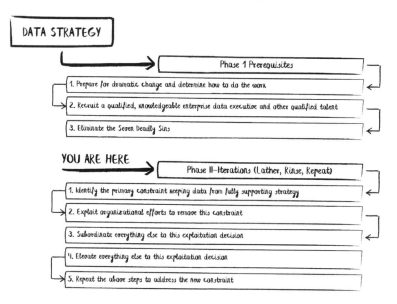

Figure 4.1 Two-phase approach to data strategy

Figure 4.1 illustrates organizational achievements as ready-to-start Phase II iterations. Each cycle represents an opportunity to improve organizational data strategy and governance practices. Phase II's continual process improvement is referred to as "lather, rinse, repeat" because it involves a deliberate programmatic effort to continually improve the way data assets are used to help facilitate the implementation of the organizational strategy. Support for the strategy is an iterative process described below.

1. Identify the biggest obstacle to leveraging data in support of organizational strategy. Eliminating this constraint will produce the greatest leverage for the benefit of the organization.

2. Formulate a plan to exploit that specific constraint.

3. Subordinate everything else to that decision.

4. Elevate that constraint to be the primary focus of organizational data governance efforts.

5. Repeat the process.

So far, we have used the phrase *data strategy iteration* to distinguish Phase II data strategy activities from the Phase I prerequisites activities. From this point, we use the phrase *data strategy*, specifically incorporating the practice of iteration. Doing so will make it easier to communicate with others involved in the process.

It is important to remember and *reinforce* that building a data strategy requires an iterative process and that each iteration represents meaningful progress toward increasing the organization's support for an enterprise data strategy. As part of this work, organizations need to be sure that leadership understands there will be multiple versions of the data strategy and that each instance represents measurable progress toward better use of data assets in support of the strategy.

It is important to remember an organization's data strategy determines how the organization defines data management, governs it and integrates it into everyday operations. In the end, the data strategy becomes the *data blueprint* or plan describing (1) how the organization will evaluate, define, plan, measure and execute a successful and mature data management program and, thereby, (2) specific leveraging of its data and people in support of organizational strategy. In this way, developing data strategies is a powerful mechanism for clarifying executive actions and decisions as well as fast-tracking the data program.

ORGANIZATIONAL STRATEGY

Good strategy requires constant, considerate and deliberate evolution, and organizations need to clearly articulate priorities in a world of seemingly unending choice. Despite appearing as an overwhelming and unachievable goal, real, tangible and sustainable differentiation is essential in an increasingly crowded and competitive arena (Daniell, 2007). For a data strategy to succeed, two things need to happen.

First, the *business* must take responsibility for developing a viable organizational strategy. For some time, organizations have been trying to solve organizational and behavioral problems with technology and ignoring the non-technological forces that are also in play. Now, perhaps more than ever, organizations need to make sure the business components remain actively involved and/or lead the organizational decision-making process, particularly as it relates to data. Strategy success depends on the *business* taking a leadership role relative to developing the organization's goals and objectives. This will not automatically solve all problems, but it will greatly help organizations effectively integrate the wide range of functions, groups and individuals involved.

Organizations need to ensure the strategy and any related decisions are shared across the organization in a manner that is clear, repeatable and understandable by all. Because strategy management effort is evolutionary, communications need be carefully crafted, well-managed and sustainable over time. Achieving business alignment evolves over time and progress is not always linear, so sustaining the data strategy requires a culture of open communication combined with a strong will to institutionalize practices that create business value and curtail or eliminate practices that do not (Carnegie Mellon University, 2014).

The organizational strategy provides guidance and direction to the data strategy. According to the Project Management Institute (2013), project sponsors or portfolio or program managers are those who typically report incongruity between organizational strategies and data strategies. When this happens, the misalignment needs to be communicated to the EDE. If the data strategy goals conflict with an established organizational strategy, it is incumbent upon the EDE to document and identify such conflicts as early as possible in the effort. Ironically, at certain times, development of an organizational strategy could be the first goal of the data strategy rather than a guiding principle. In such a case, it is important for the data strategy to specifically define what constitutes an appropriate organizational strategy that will sustain the organization.

Organizational strategy is typically hierarchically arranged as shown in Figure 4.2.

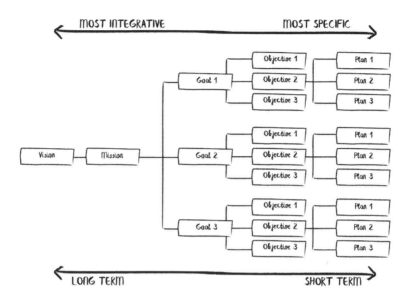

Figure 4.2 Strategic planning hierarchy

While strategy development involves people, resources and time, it also requires documentation: the recording of issues, considerations and decisions leaders make and which ultimately help the organization reach a desired state and strategic position. Strategy development and its accompanying documentation become central to several tasks the organization performs. Those tasks include strategic planning, strategy implementation and strategic control (Grunig, 2015). Based on this definition, a *strategy* may be characterized by the following features.

- Contains long-term guidelines, normally fixed in the form of documents or more often presentation slides.

- Relates to the organization or to important parts.

- Is set by management.

- Reflects successes that are built and maintained.

- Guarantees sustainment of values, goals and objectives.

SUPPORTING ORGANIZATIONAL STRATEGY WITH DATA STRATEGY

Most organizations adopt what initially seems to be a reasonable approach to implementing an organizational data strategy (see, Figure 4.3).

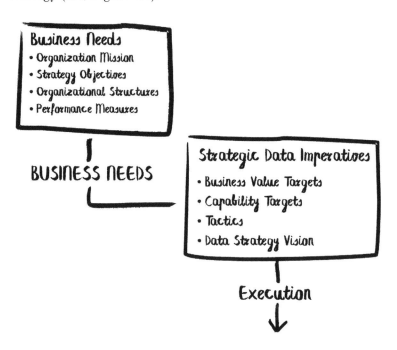

Figure 4.3 A typical approach to data strategy

Organizations need to carefully review their needs, match specific data planning components and implement them. While this approach may appear reasonable, it omits a crucial dimension: the current state of organizational data maturity. Because data maturity is often so low (Aiken & Gillenson, 2011), attempting to implement a process or technical capability inevitably leads to disappointment and wasteful spending. These efforts have the same unacceptably low success rates as most information technology projects.

Recall that a strategic outcome is a result of a pattern in a stream of decisions. Technologies represent a component of what the P3T need to address organizational progress. For example, MDM is often offered as a data strategy when, in fact, it is not. It is an important program that is part of a larger data strategy. Despite this, however, vendors routinely package and market MDM solutions as data strategy. This is an example of vendors promoting technical solutions to address what is fundamentally a business problem. Below is a description of how these efforts typically proceed.

An organization decided to develop a data strategy. As part of this work, the organization realized some of its data was more important than others. With outside assistance, the organization concluded that an MDM solution would solve the problem. After the organization invested millions of dollars in the MDM solution, the IT team moved on because the project was finished, and the organization incurred the usual cost and schedule overruns. After time passed, the organization observed that things were not getting better, and some began to ask where they should put their data. Lacking clear direction, someone decided to put it "into the MDM." Though the IT team implemented the MDM solution according to specifications, the organization received little or no benefit from the technology because the organization failed to implement data quality and data governance prior to the technical solution.

When organizations buy technical solutions for problems they do not understand that this is analogous to handing the keys of a Tesla to a new driver and expecting that individual to know how to operate a complex, high-performance vehicle. What do you think will happen?

It is very difficult to imagine that organizations would ever achieve desirable outcomes if they work this way. Jonathan Sacks (2012) offers some insight that helps us understand the problem. Sacks notes that, while technology gives people power, it does not and cannot tell them how to use that power. Sacks adds, "Thanks to technology, we can instantly communicate across the world, but it still doesn't help us know what to say." It is key to remember that there are no shortcuts—organizations need to build the foundational competencies in data and associated foundational disciplines before they can hope to benefit from it. Otherwise, they will be simply making mistakes at the speed of light.

Equally important is the fact that technical solutions need to be aligned with the organization's data maturity. In other words, utilize technology that organizations understand, particularly as it relates to automating data processes. When this happens, organizations will always produce better results. Consequently, organizations need to plan the introduction of data capabilities in organizational data strategies when they make sense and are understood by those who will be performing those duties. Lack of organizational maturity accounts for many of what are routinely written off as IT failures.

We have referenced the DMM several times so far, and now we need to provide some context around this phrase. While all improvement efforts begin with the obligatory "assessment" phase, Carnegie Mellon's CMMI and DMM are the only proven frameworks that have the added benefit of literally decades of research, practice, and benchmarking data (Board, 2006). Organizations not using the DMM risk an inability to meaningfully compare results against other organizations and, as a result, adopt unproven methods.

Figure 4.4 illustrates the correct process for determining whether an organization's strategic data imperatives are correctly derived from matches with its organizational needs and current capabilities.

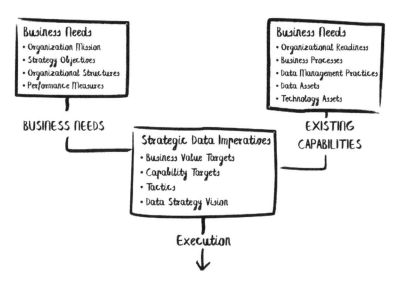

Figure 4.4 A better approach to data strategy

An effective data strategy describes why the organization is implementing data management program features and improvements. It explains what the overall program aims to achieve and identifies how the various components fit together. To this end, data assets can best be employed to support organizational business objectives if it is done in an iterative fashion. Working this way will help organizations identify and mitigate risks earlier. It will allow organizations to change operating tactics when requirements change. It will help organizations continually improve and refine products, and it will help organizations learn in a controlled manner, allowing them to improve their processes without catastrophic consequences to the organization and its business.

It is important to note, too, that *the data strategy development process is subordinate to the organizational strategy and not to the IT strategy*. This is a very difficult concept to understand and respect. Many instinctively realize that the organizational strategy provides guidance and direction to the data strategy. However, many do not. The key to a successful data strategy is to first align data with the organizational strategy and then have IT align its strategy with the data needs.

Each iteration of the data strategy needs to accurately reflect business requirements to give stakeholders confidence that the data management program is valuable, practical and always managed with business equities in mind. Moreover, data strategy emphasizes the importance of collaboration as well as the specific data challenges that derive from the interconnected nature of business processes. Each iteration defines the overall framework of the data management program, describes how the plan should be structured to address the core principles of data management and is communicated to critical stakeholders so they can understand the value of a data management program as it relates to their functions and strategic initiatives. Furthermore, since data strategy is not static, it must be able to evolve as the needs of the organization change.

Figure 4.5 illustrates a single iteration of a data strategy development cycle. (Our colleague, Lewis Broome, contributed to articulation of this model.) It is also important to note that, at the end of each iteration, organizations should realize increased business value *and* have new organizational data capabilities that could be communicated to the organization and offered as *quick wins*. However, if organizations spend too much focusing on technical capabilities, management will often declare the work to be a science project or something that fails to yield concrete results. Conversely, if organizations focus too much on achieving business value, management regularly

concludes that the effort inhibits the organization's ability to
develop new capabilities.

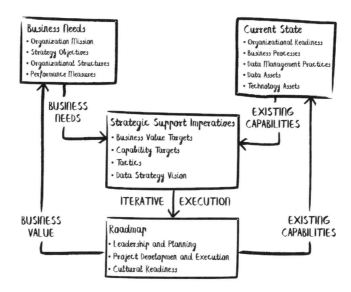

Figure 4.5 A balanced data strategy iteration cycle-general form

Iterative development will and should, always be a constrained
optimization problem. So, let us take a moment and review this
situation using the constraints maximization framework. To
achieve the requisite balance in these areas, we adapt a proven
and popular approach first postulated by Eliyahu Goldratt.

GOLDRATT'S THEORY OF CONSTRAINTS

While there are many different frameworks that organizations
can use to structure a discussion about strategy, we base ours on
the most widely known and practiced framework. The *Theory of
Constraints* has been taught, read, watched and heard more
than any competing theory, framework or method (Goldratt,
1984). The theory's strength is in its simplicity and common
sense approach to problem-solving which is essentially: discover

the most important challenge that is preventing the organization from achieving its goals, fix it and move to the next (lather, rinse, repeat).

Academia has been using this framework in the classroom for some time, and its popularity in industry is unchallenged. Besides being the best-known method—and more importantly, already popular with management, Goldratt's *system* is the easiest to understand. Goldratt suggested systems were like chains or a network of chains. Each chain is composed of links that differ in function and strength, and each chain contains one, and only one, link that is weaker than all the others. See Figure 4.6.

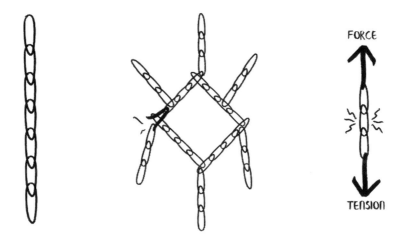

Figure 4.6 System as chains - one weak link in each dependent chain

The weakest link limits the performance of the entire chain. Simply put, the weakest link is a *constraint* to overall system performance. If one takes steps to strengthen the weakest link, that link will no longer be the weakest link; some other link would, in turn, become the weakest link.

The basic idea behind Goldratt's theory is that all processes have at least one constraint associated with it, and the overall throughput of the system can only be improved when constraints are improved or eliminated. A related and equally important concept posits that the amount of time one spends optimizing non-constraints will not provide significant improvement.

Goldratt's method offers organizations several benefits:

- improved process throughput of a product or service;

- increased profitability resulting from throughput goal achievement;

- increased productivity, capacity and quality;

- reduced lead times and inventory levels;

- improved customer satisfaction; and

- improved culture, employee engagement and problem-solving.

The *Theory of Constraints* uses Five Focusing Steps to identify and eliminate constraints (Figure 4.7).

The first step is to identify the current constraints, the parts of the system that limit the rate at which a goal is realized. Once that is accomplished, organizations make quick improvements to the constraint using existing resources. They then review other activities in the process to facilitate proper alignment and support of constraint. If, after this, the constraint persists, organizations review what other actions could be taken to eliminate the constraint. This step repeats until the constraint is eliminated.

In some cases, organizations may need to make focused capital investments to eliminate the constraint. Afterward, the organization engages the next constraint. Though Goldratt developed the *Theory of Constraints* for manufacturing, it provides an appropriate model to assist in development of an organization's data strategy.

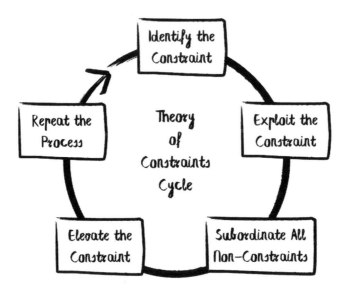

Figure 4.7 **Five focusing steps for identifying and eliminating constraints**

Objectives of the constraint management process are to develop the overall constraint management plan for the organization, to decide how the constraint management processes will be executed and to integrate constraint management with other data management activities. The cost of treating the constraints themselves should be included appropriately in data management, while the constraint management plan should describe how this part of the data management budget is evaluated, allocated and managed.

The data strategy demonstrates the business value that the program will seek to achieve, and, in the end, the data strategy becomes the blueprint or plan describing how the organization will evaluate, define, plan, measure and execute a successful and mature data management program.

The data strategy defines the overall framework of the data management program and should be structured to address the core principles of data management. In this way, critical stakeholders can understand the value of a data management program as it relates to their functions and strategic initiatives.

IDENTIFYING ORGANIZATIONAL DATA CONSTRAINTS

A constraint cannot be managed unless it is first identified. Consequently, after constraint management planning has been completed, organizations need to identify all knowable constraints to the data strategy. The purpose of constraint identification is to identify current data restrictions, those constraints that impede strategic progress. The fact that some constraints are unknowable or emergent means that constraint identification should be iterative, identifying constraints that surface with each iteration. When organizations identify constraints, they should also identify candidate responses for each constraint at the same time. Organizations need to record candidate responses as part of the constraint response process.

Organizations also need to refrain from focusing on local areas of the system and, instead, identify and isolate bottlenecks that affect the entire system. Working this way requires a clear understanding of the organizational strategy, and it is important that organizations understand and respect their capabilities, limitations, strengths and weaknesses before rushing in and selecting and implementing tools and methods. Some tools that may be used as part of this work include Pareto analysis, flow charts, process maps, scorecards, RACI[5] matrices, SIPOC[6] diagrams, root-cause analysis, cause-and-effect diagrams, affinity diagrams, brainstorming, multi-voting and the nominal group technique. One popular tool for identifying bottlenecks and other issues is the SWOT model, which assesses strengths, weaknesses, opportunities and threats.

Originally known as the *SOFT[7] Model*, Albert Humphrey is credited for creating the SWOT model while working at Stanford University in the 1960s and 1970s. SWOT is another model that helps systematically identify and quantify internal and external factors that affect an organization's ability to be successful (Pahl & Richter, 2009). Perhaps Graham, Friend and Stefan Zehle (2004) described it best: a SWOT analysis supports understanding of strengths and weaknesses in the context of opportunities and threats. Additionally, SWOT provides another way to evaluate forces internal and external to an organization (McQuaig, 2007).

Results of a SWOT analysis are essential to making improvements to an organization, helping to close gaps among other elements for effective and efficient decision-making. According to Michael Gendron (2014), as organizations begin various initiatives, they often have to determine the best and most appropriate strategies, articulate goals and objectives, identify discriminating competencies and assess organizational strengths, weaknesses, opportunities and threats within a

---

[5] responsible, accountable, consulted, informed

[6] supply, input, process, output, customer

[7] satisfactory, opportunity, fault, threat

competitive environment. A sample SWOT analysis summary is shown at Figure 4.8.

Once organizations conduct environmental scans, specifically recording weaknesses and threats, they can identify constraints and develop plans to remove them. A key concept here is that, when organizations eliminate any constraint, they are not finished; instead, they need to perform the scan again and again. Doing so will slowly but steadily reduce the organization's constraints and position it for success.

SWOT ANALYSIS TEMPLATE Assessment For: New Business Opportunity			
Criteria Examples Advantages of Proposition Capabilities Competitive Advantages Unique Selling Points (USP) Resources, Assets, People Experience, Knowledge, Data Financial Reserves, Likely Returns Marketing Reach, Distribution, Awareness Innovative Aspects Location and Geography Price, Value, Quality Accreditations, Qualifications, Certifications Processes, Systems, IT, Communications	**STRENGTHS** Well positioned for contract award. Hold innovative patents. Have inside knowledge of customer space. Have offices already near customer. Offer competitive pricing.	**WEAKNESSES** Missing key component for enterprise solution. Minimal budget to support proposal effort of this scale. Pressure from board of directors to win. Minimal accreditations for key staff.	**Criteria Examples** Disadvantages of Proposition Gaps in Capabilities Lack of Competitive Strength Reputation, Presence and Reach Financials Own Known Vulnerabilities Timescales, Deadlines, and Pressures Cash Flow, Start-Up Cash-Drain Continuity, Supply Chain Robustness Effects on Core Activities, Destruction Reliability of Data, Plan Predictability Morale, Commitment, Leadership Accreditations
Criteria Examples Market Developments Competitor's Vulnerabilities Industry or Lifestyle Trends Technology Development and Innovation Global Influences New Markets, Vertical, Horizontal Niche Target Markets Geographical, Export, Import New USP's Tactics: Surprise, Major Contacts Business and Product Development Information and Research Partnerships, Agencies	**OPPORTUNITIES** Have good insight into competition. New technology almost complete. Growing demand by third-party players. Could offer technology as part of bid.	**THREATS** Strong competition in existing space. Legislation under consideration in Congress could affect eligibility. Strong incumbent support from customer.	**Criteria Examples** Political Effects Legislative Effects Environmental Effects IT Developments Competitor Intentions Market Demand New Technologies, Services, Ideas Vital Contracts and Partners Sustaining Internal Capabilities Obstacles Faced Insurmountable Weaknesses Loss of Key Staff Sustainable Financial Backing Economy, Home, Abroad Seasonality, Weather Effects

Figure 4.8 Sample SWOT analysis for new business opportunity

EXPLOITING ORGANIZATIONAL DATA CONSTRAINTS

The term "exploit" may seem a little strange to many. The term is not negative. What Goldratt means is that organizations need to do whatever they can to optimize every capability available. Organizations should consider what can be done to improve or eliminate constraints without having to make expensive investments. Some simple things include removing non-value work, removing or limiting interruptions, allowing resources to work at a steady pace and providing higher quality tools and materials.

When exploiting constraints, organizations need to carefully prioritize work so they are always focusing on the most important bottlenecks. Good recordkeeping means that the organization takes overall responsibility and reviews and approves all work that the organization performs. Additionally, change measurements should be taken as bottlenecks relative to the entire system are improved and eliminated. With each change made to the constraint, organizations need to measure change at the system level to affirm that the made are, in fact, improving system throughput rather than hindering it. Last, special attention should be given to critical constraints to ensure those key resources are always busy and not idle. For example, if an operator takes a scheduled break, make sure someone has back-filled for that individual so production can continue.

SUBORDINATING ALL OTHER CONSTRAINTS

According to Michael Dettmer (1998), the weakest link will set the pace for work. After the constraint has been identified and the team has determined how to optimize it, synchronize it with other system components. When this happens, there is almost always a need to optimize different parts of the system. This could include adjusting rates of other activities in the process so they are aligned with constraint.

It is important to note that this might slow other activities elsewhere within the system. Although seeming odd or even counterintuitive to many, it is important to measure how individual changes affect the overall throughput of the system. In some instances, such system behavior may run contrary to some organizational reward systems.

When organizations decide to fully exploit bottlenecks, they must subordinate every other decision. Any other resources that aren't bottlenecked have, by definition, some slack. Use that slack to support the bottleneck. Organizations need to be sure they are not applying too many resources to the constraint. Otherwise, work will build up around the bottleneck and exacerbate the problem.

For example, if organizations were tuning a production process and engineers determined a specific machine was a bottleneck, the team would not overload the machine with additional work or resources assigned to correct the problem. Instead, the team would work to ensure the machine was working at 100 percent capacity, and they would tune the machine's performance in a way that improved the overall system throughput.

Most managers are evaluated on efficiency—not effectiveness—of their people. Deliberately making people work below capacity goes against goals achievement. This problem can be solved by fully loading the non-bottlenecks while ensuring that at least a part of the work is non-essential: nice if it gets done, but not immediately necessary or time-critical. Whenever the non-bottlenecks need to support the bottleneck, they can drop the non-essential work to free up time. Such organizations may need to change practices and policies to make sure the organization is getting the most from every constraint.

ELEVATING ORGANIZATIONAL DATA CONSTRAINTS

At some point, managers will have to make decisions about bottlenecks. Did remediation steps improve the constraint? Is overall throughput of the system improved? While the exploitation and subordination steps are often sufficient, there are instances when they are not. When this happens, organizations will have to increase capacity of the constrained parts of the process until the bottleneck is improved or eliminated.

For example, if an organization determined a certain machine was the weakest link, the team might decide to purchase more modern or better equipment. The organization might also decide to change the production schedule and let another shift handle the extra work. In other cases, the organization may decide to provide training and mentoring rather than switching technologies. Thus, *elevating* means making capital investments while resolving a system problem.

Elevation improvements are more difficult because they require an investment. They are also risky as most of these improvements take time before they produce results. In this situation, it is important to remember the old saying: it is going to get worse before it gets better. For the EDE, this is particularly important. The EDE needs to be able to manage expectations and make sure leadership understands some time will elapse before improvements start to have a positive effect. For example, when an organization adds new people to a team, the team does not immediately become more effective. What happens, instead, is that the new team members lower the team's velocity, and, as a result, the team needs to accept less work while the team helps the new teammates get up to speed.

REPEATING THE PROCESS

After organizations improve or eliminate bottlenecks, they need to step back, look at the system and identify the new weakest link. When a new bottleneck is identified, improvement must be implemented, as before. Realize that this is a never-ending cycle of repair and improvement. With each successive cycle, individual system components change; what was the weakest link becomes productive again; what was once broken now works. These simple yet powerful steps focus on optimizing system performance by focusing on specific components and measuring performance relative to overall system throughput.

MANAGING DATA CONSTRAINTS

The following discussion describes a structured approach to understanding and managing data constraints within organizations. As discussed above, constraints are forces that limit an organization's ability to successfully meet its goals and objectives. Specifically, data constraints have a negative effect on the organization and its work. From this perspective, constraints exist in relation to objectives. It is, then, essential to clearly identify such constraints so that options can be carefully considered for mitigating or eliminating the constraints entirely. It is also clear that different organizations are exposed to different kinds of constraints, so each step in the constraint management process should be scalable to meet the varying degrees of constraints.

In order to manage system constraints, organizations need to have a plan that describes how different parts of the organization would identify, assess, abate, monitor and control constraints across the enterprise (Project Management Institute, 2009). The objectives of the constraint management process are to develop an overall constraint management plan for the organization, to decide how constraint management process will be executed and to integrate constraint management with other data management activities.

The plan describes how the constraint management processes should be carried out and how each component of the plan aligns with the other data management processes. In a broader sense, the constraint management process describes relationships among constraint management, general data management and business processes that exist across the organization. Corresponding constraint management activities should be integrated into the overall data improvement plan. The constraint management plan may subsequently need to be adapted as organizational and stakeholder needs of the organization become more clear or change.

Although the constraint management processes form an integral part of the overall data management plan, a budget in terms of resources, cost and time to execute the specific constraint management activities should be established in order to better track, control and, as necessary, defend the corresponding expenditures throughout the project. The cost of treating the constraints themselves should be included appropriately in the data management program, while the constraint management plan should describe how this part of the data management budget is evaluated, allocated and managed.

The constraint management plan will define monitoring methods to ensure corresponding expenditures are tracked appropriately, as well as the conditions under which the approved budget for constraint management can be modified. In the same way that data management is a process of progressive elaboration, constraint management activities need to be repeated across data management activities. The constraint management plan should define both the normal frequency for repeating the processes and specific or exceptional conditions under which the corresponding actions are to be initiated.

ELEMENTS OF A DATA STRATEGY

A data strategy typically includes a vision statement, goals and objectives, priorities, scope, defined business benefits, a data management framework, high-level roles and responsibilities and governance needs. It will frequently include a description of the approach used to develop the data management program, the high-level compliance approach and measures and a high-level sequence plan (roadmap).

A data strategy usually consists, at a minimum of the following elements.

1) **Version:** Whole number changes represent iterations with iteration improvements and clarifications indicated to the right of the iteration cycle number, (i.e., 4.3 represents the third version of the fourth iteration).

2) **Vision:** Concerned with what the organization aspires to be, its purpose is to set out a view of the future to enthuse, gain commitment from and improve the performances of its workers (Johnson, 2011).

3) **Mission:** The overall purpose and raison d'être of the organization is developed and communicated to employees and stakeholders (Johnson, 2011).

4) **Goals:** Open-ended statements describe what one wishes to accomplish in pursuit of the mission with no quantification of what is to be achieved and no timeframe for completion (Hill, 2011).

5) **Objectives:** Statements as to what activity is to be accomplished in pursuit of desired end results, and related timelines, are established to support achievement of goals. They should be quantified if possible (Hill, 2011).

6) **Plan:** To implement established policy, a statement that prescribes specific actions to be is developed (Project Management Institute, 2016).

7) **Priorities:** In line with its definition, hierarchical consideration is assigned to competing alternatives. (Merriam Webster, 2016).

8) **Scope:** As indication of the "whole" to be addressed, the sum of products, services and results to be provided as a project are outlined. See also "project scope" and "product scope" (Project Management Institute, 2013).

Data strategy needs to reinforce the use of standards and outline the overall governance framework an organization will utilize regarding implementation decision-making. The data strategy should also reflect major implementation considerations, such as architectural initiatives and technology transformation initiatives that are underway or planned, and it needs to define a sequence plan to guide implementation.

The data strategy iterations must evolve as the needs of the organization change. Organizations will be able to affect change through close collaboration of different organizational components. Collaboration is essential to building and maintaining an effective data management program. One example of improved collaboration is a broader responsibility for data quality led by executives and reflected throughout the data lifecycle. The most effective data management strategies are those that are visibly and actively endorsed by executive management and supported by mandatory organizational policy. In effect, such strategies are institutionalized.

The ensuing collaborative project—developing the data strategy—is a powerful mechanism for clarifying executive decisions and directives, as well as fast-tracking the data management program. In the ideal instance, all key players have had a voice in the process. They have reached agreement on objectives, priorities and measures. They have secured executive approval for capabilities to be improved, and all relevant stakeholders understand the impacts of the plan.

In organizations that are "born digital" or "become digital," digital strategy and organizational strategy might be one and the same. However, we recognize that the challenges of the current transitional period from the older, analog world to the 21st century digital world and beyond often create the need for parallel development of strategy components.

WHO CONTRIBUTES TO THE DATA STRATEGY?

The EDE is the individual responsible for producing the organization's data strategy. However, this person cannot develop the plan alone. It is critical that the EDE involve other members of the organization so all equities are considered going forward (see Figure 4.9).

Stakeholders include all members of the strategy team, as well as all interested parties internal and external to the organization. The data strategy team identifies the positive and negative forces involved and manages the influences of these various stakeholders (Project Management Institute, 2013). Specifically, the team ensures that they closely collaborate with stakeholders to make sure that management data strategy requirements and expectations of all parties involved are met.

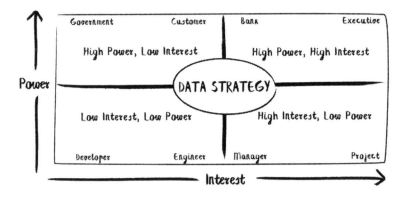

Figure 4.9 Stakeholder analysis for producing a data strategy

Additionally, creating an effective data strategy requires the involvement of key stakeholders working from a sound base of careful research into internal capabilities and external factors that could affect the organization's business. Using the *Theory of Constraints* model, senior management utilizes this information to identify top priority issues (constraints) that the organization must address to be successful. Organizations then create action plans for each item as well as a set of procedures for implementing them. Because developing an effective strategy requires time, reflection and constant two-way communication with senior management, collaboration between business leaders, and even customers and other key stakeholders, it facilitates buy-in and alignment of the data strategy. Two-way communication will also provide management with honest feedback, insights and a more genuine perspective of organizations and their data.

So, what is a stakeholder in practical terms? A *stakeholder* is an individual, group or organization that may affect, be affected by or perceive itself to be affected by a decision, activity or outcome of a project. Examples of business stakeholders who have a stake in the effort are listed below.

- plant operators
- manufacturing line supervisors
- help desk staff
- production system support analysts
- customer service representatives
- salespersons
- maintenance workers
- telephone sales personnel
- call center personnel
- retail workers
- line managers
- training officers

Stakeholders may be actively involved in the data strategy development process or have interests that may be positively or negatively affected by the performance or completion of the work. Different stakeholders may have competing expectations that might create conflicts within the data strategy. Stakeholders may also exert influence over the strategy development, its deliverables and the strategy team in order to achieve a set of outcomes that satisfy their specific strategic business objectives or other organizational needs.

DEVELOPING A DATA STRATEGY

Recall that the best results are obtained when organizational needs are matched to the current ability of the organization to take advantage of strategic data imperatives. A specific example occurs when organizations build metadata repository capabilities before investing millions of dollars in a packaged solution. By learning from its experiences with the yearlong practice session with a home-grown solution, organizations will be in an experientially stronger position to have conversations with the vendor community than they would have been without the *practice year*.

Similarly, the organization's approach to implementation of specific initiatives must be balanced between delivering tangible business value and new organizational capabilities. Imbalance toward capabilities will make the exercise appear as a science project, and too much emphasis on business value will not provide the organization the needed capabilities and maturation required to meet the capabilities of the technologies provided by the vendor community.

When developing a data strategy, it is critical to incorporate seven specific elements. Each is considered below.

1. UNDERSTANDING THE ENVIRONMENT

The environment is what gives organizations the means of survival. In the private sector, satisfied customers are what keep organizations in business. In the public sector, it is government, clients, patients or students whom are the stakeholders that give meaning to governments and other institutions (Johnson, 2011). However, the environment is also the source of threats. For example, hostile shifts in market demand, new regulatory requirements, revolutionary technologies or the entry of new competitors can easily affect the environment and those organizations operating within it.

The environment is agnostic to organizations. It can provide infinite opportunity and success, but it can also be fatal for those same organizations if they do not understand the forces at work in the environment. To understand the environment, organizations need to analyze various aspects, including internal and external factors, that are variables in the organizations' consideration formulas. There are several stages that make up the analytical phase. Sometimes referred to as the discovery, assessment and current-state phase, this analysis provides a snapshot of an organization's ecosystem (Nichols, 2015).

For this element, organizations survey business goals, existing content, competitive content, content operations, content life cycles and governance structures. This analysis provides a detailed understanding of how content performs and functions in the current environment. Such understanding provides a foundation for an improved, future-state model. By identifying gaps, issues, pain points, strengths and requirements within the current state, content strategists can determine how the content ecosystem functions within organizations and how they need to change.

2. DEVELOPING DATA VISION FOR ORGANIZATIONAL STRATEGY

The first step in producing a data strategy is setting the vision for organizational use of data. The organizational strategy should be the springboard for developing data strategy. The data strategy should include statements of organizational business values and culture and, when using the organizational strategy, describe the desired information state to support the organization.

3. DETERMINING THE IMPACT OF THE VISION

Identify what will be different because of the information vision. Describe what the desired end state means to the organization. Explain in specific terms the differences between the current information state and the desired information state. Compare characteristics of the current state to the target state—side-by-side—to accentuate the differences. This will engender clear thought about the work's necessary streams, key milestones and deliverables. Along the way, ask yourself questions such as, "How will the future state affect profitability, market position, customer satisfaction and support?"

4. IDENTIFYING THE REQUISITE BUSINESS PROCESSES

This section describes the business processes organizations must implement to be successful. Identify how the information processes will support the business vision. Describe what is different about the new processes. Also, determine who will be responsible for performing each process. This will help identify which stakeholders need to be involved. Identify performance measures related to performance in each process.

5. DEVELOPING MISSION STATEMENTS FOR DATA STRATEGY

The data strategy mission statement is the foremost corporate document (Grunig, 2015). It has three important characteristics:

- A mission statement does not include any specific time limit for its validity. It will need to be revised or replaced if it obstructs the success of the organization because of changes in the environment or in the organization itself.

- A mission statement is composed of a thread of interrelated principles. A principle is defined here as a prescriptive statement that limits, to a greater or lesser extent, the space within which certain categories of decisions may be made.

- A data strategy mission statement creates a framework for the future development of data improvements. The guidelines set out in the mission statement must be respected when developing strategy components. However, it also includes issues that are not of primary relevance to strategic planning but mainly affect other areas. Examples would be statements concerning staff development or principles concerning the use of natural resources.

6. LINKING THE VISION AND MISSION WITH BUSINESS VALUES

Many organizations have developed a set of values to guide the actions and behavior of organization personnel in conducting the organization's business and pursuing its strategic vision and mission (Thompson, 2012). *Values* (or "core values," as they are often called) are certain designated beliefs, traits and behavioral norms that leadership has determined should guide the pursuit of its vision and mission. Values relate to such things as fair treatment, honor and integrity, ethical behavior, innovativeness, teamwork, a passion for top-notch quality or superior customer service, social responsibility and community citizenship.

7. SETTING THE OBJECTIVES

Most organizations articulate four to eight core values personnel are expected to display and that are supposed to be mirrored in how organizations conduct their business (Thompson, 2012). At organizations where the stated values are real rather than cosmetic, managers connect values to the pursuit of the strategic vision and mission in one of two ways. The managerial purpose of setting objectives is to convert the vision and mission into specific performance targets. Objectives reflect management's aspirations for organizational performance in light of the industry's prevailing economic and competitive conditions and the organization's internal capabilities. Well-stated objectives must be specific, quantifiable or measurable and challenging, and they must contain a deadline for achievement.

In organizations with values that are deeply entrenched in the corporate culture, senior managers are careful to craft a vision, a mission, a strategy and set of operating practices that match established values. Moreover, they repeatedly emphasize how the value-based behavioral norms contribute to the organization's business success. If the organization changes its vision or strategy, executives take care to explain how and why core values continue to be relevant. Few organizations with sincere commitment to established core values ever undertake strategic moves that conflict with ingrained values.

MANAGING THE STRATEGY DEVELOPMENT PROCESS

Projects are temporary endeavors undertaken to create a unique product, service or result. The temporary nature of projects indicates a project has a definite beginning and end (see Figure 4.10). The end is reached when the project's objectives have been achieved, when the project is terminated because its objectives will not or cannot be met or when the need for the project no longer exists. A project may also be terminated if the client, customer, sponsor or champion wishes to terminate the project.

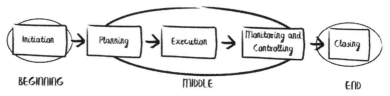

BEGINNING   **MIDDLE**   **END**

Figure 4.10 Project lifecycle

A group of related projects, subprograms and program activities may be managed in a coordinated way to obtain benefits not available from managing them individually. Programs are comprised of various components, most of these being individual projects within the program. Programs may also include other work related to the component projects, such as training, operations and maintenance activities.

Projects are often utilized as a means of directly or indirectly achieving objectives within an organization's strategic plan. Projects are typically authorized because of one or more of the following strategic considerations exist.

- market demand (e.g., a car manufacturer authorizing a project to build more fuel-efficient cars in response to gasoline shortages)

- strategic opportunity or business need (e.g., a training organization authorizing a project to create a new course to increase its revenues)

- social need (e.g., a nongovernmental organization in a developing country authorizing a project to provide potable water systems, latrines and sanitation education to communities suffering from high rates of infectious diseases)

- environmental consideration (e.g., a public organization authorizing a project to create a new service for electric car sharing to reduce pollution)

- customer request (e.g., an electric utility authorizing a project to build a new substation to serve a new industrial park)

- technological advance (e.g., an electronics manufacturer authorizing a new project to develop a faster, cheaper, smaller laptop based on advances in computer memory and electronics technology)

- legal requirement (e.g., a chemical manufacturer authorizing a project to establish guidelines for proper handling of a new toxic material)

COMMUNICATING AND DATA STRATEGY

While many organizations have a solid strategy, they may not share it in a way the workforce fully understands and appreciates. Ensuring that everyone understands where the organization is going is a very difficult thing to do. In communicating with the appropriate parties, the organization sends signals to stakeholders, individuals and groups who have an interest in the organization and who may wish to influence or play a role in aspects of its mission, objectives and strategies.

In its simplest form, communication is *storytelling*. These are stories describing human achievement and a combination of individual and collaborative successes and failures. Such stories are filled with drama, meaning and often humor. Those telling stories are constantly challenged to make the stories engaging and compelling. Storytellers do this by making each story concrete and specific. When told, stories help people develop relationships among individuals and ideas. The stories should be sure to include internal and external audiences and should never be shared as a one-shot deal. According to researcher Gary Marx (2006), stories (i.e., communications) should be told on a continuous basis—all the time.

For some stakeholders and organizations, communications can be more effective if they include in-person events (e.g., regular meetings, structured workshops, town hall events). The mechanisms, frequency and timing of communications are typically captured in a communications plan. In addition, communications requiring action or a response are more likely to be effective when they come from senior management (Carnegie Mellon University, 2014). Let us expand on a few of these.

SENDING THE RIGHT MESSAGE TO THE RIGHT PEOPLE

The first step in a communication plan is to identify and segment the audiences and to customize or modify the message to the degree that is necessary to be effective. Communications to IT team can have a more technical slant; communications to legal teams can have some legal jargon and emphasize legal issues. The more forethought one puts into crafting a communications strategy, the more effective it will be (Smallwood, 2014).

Researchers Gerry Johnson, Kevin Scholes and Richard Whittington (2011) offer additional recommendations for communicating strategic information throughout organizations.

- **Focus.** Communications should be focused on the key components of the strategy, avoiding unnecessary detail or complex language. For example, CEO Jack Welch's famous statement that General Electric should be "either Number One or Number Two" in all its markets is remembered precisely because of this clear focus on the importance of being a dominant player wherever the company competed (Johnson et al, 2011).

- **Impact.** Communications should be impactful, with powerful and memorable words and visuals. For example, the United Kingdom's new community services strategy is powerfully titled "Our health, our care, our say" to embody the inclusiveness and direct importance of the strategy for all citizens.

- **Media.** Choosing appropriate media to convey the new strategy is very important. Mass media such as e-mails, voicemails, company newsletters, videos, intranets and senior manager blogs can ensure all staff receive the same message promptly, helping to avoid damaging uncertainty and rumor mongering. However, face-to-face communications are important, too, to demonstrate the personal commitment of managers and allow for interaction with concerned staff. Thus, senior managers may undertake roadshows, carrying their message directly to various groups of employees with conferences or workshops at different sites.

- **Employee Engagement.** It is often helpful to engage employees directly in the strategy, so they can see what it means for them personally and how their role will change. Interchanges through roadshows and cascades can help, but some organizations use imaginative means to create more active engagement.

COMMUNICATING ALL THE TIME

Marx (2006) also noted that for strategies to truly be successful, communication must be effective, pervasive and a part of everything people do. Marx adds that communication helps people come together so they can exchange ideas and that future-focused communication requires people to make even more effective use of critical and creative thinking skills.

Truly astute, forward-looking organizations often include effective communication among their goals and key objectives. Whatever our organization, we should ensure that open, honest and strategic communication is supported by policy and considered important in the budget. Marx offers some very practical advice when communicating strategic ideas.

- **Get connected to the world of ideas.** Unfortunately, when we think of communication in an organization, we too often consider it to be only writing, speaking and working with the news media, all of which are important. However, strategic, future-focused communication requires us to make even more intense use of our critical and creative thinking skills (Marx, 2006). Our aim is to be constantly connected with the internal and external environments and to consider how to make sense of the complexity that has become an ongoing part of a fast-moving society.

- **Involve internal and external stakeholders.** The typical process begins with organizations identifying their key internal and external stakeholders, identifying what they need to know and developing a plan for making sure they each stay informed and involved.

- **Be sure communication is ongoing.** To be effective, communication must be a continuous process reinforced by a wide assortment of vehicles, processes and programs. Some of these tools include newsletters, websites, meetings, reports, news media, training, formal and informal opinion polls and much more. Make communication a part of everything the organization does.

COMMUNICATING DATA STRATEGY

Data strategy must begin with the *why* ahead of the *how* and *what*, but while this seems obvious to many, most organizations do not follow this guidance. Instead, they plunge headlong into protracted strategy development without first understanding the forces involved and how they interact with one another. By concentrating communications, messaging and resources on their motivation (why), organizations can improve the quality of communication and benefit from clarity of intent as others design the processes (how) for implementing the true mission of the organization. Similarly, with an organization aligned to its true purpose, well-designed processes can be leveraged to effectively and efficiently produce the organization's desired outcomes (what).

To help better understand this phenomenon, we present a model for large organizations which clearly illustrates the disconnect between the organizational strategy and specific IT projects. While organizations may have thoughtful and unambiguous strategies, organizations regularly share their plans in a manner like the Chinese Whispers game, and, as different people share their understanding of the plan with others, different things happen. Some people do not communicate the message at all. They keep it to themselves. Others go around other parts of the organization, skipping the middle and communicating directly with lower level organizational components. Still other people go completely outside their organizational boundaries and share different versions of the plan with others. When this kind of communication happens at scale across the entire organization, people quickly become confused and frustrated.

Sadly, this is common among many organizations. We have noted that this is particularly problematic for IT organizations where, despite the best intentions, they fail to align IT work with the organizational strategy.

To illustrate this problem, recall the game, Telephone, that you may have played when you were young. This game is an excellent example of the unreliability of even the simplest communications and the process by which most organizations disseminate information and strategies. Telephone (aka Chinese Whispers), excellently demonstrates the unreliability of verbal communications. A referee lines up all the players in a straight line or circle so each person can only communicate with the person directly next to them. The game begins when the first person whispers a phrase as quietly as possible to the person directly next to him. The recipient listens carefully and then shares what was heard with the next person on his opposite side. This continues until the last person in line gets the message. When the last player gets the message, this person tells the referee what they heard. The referee compares the original message with the last (Adams Media, 2015).

The entertainment comes from comparing the original and final messages and learning how distorted even the simplest message becomes when it is shared person-to-person. Pause here for a moment and reflect on what this means for more complicated messages. If even the simplest messages become distorted, what is the likelihood a complicated message would remain intact when shared in this manner? What do you think this would do to your organizational strategy?

The bottom line is that communicating is immensely difficult, and the simpler you make your strategy, the more likely everyone will receive it, understand it and apply it to their relative position in the organization (Figure 4.11). These same principles are true for data strategies, as well.

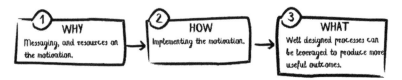

Figure 4.11 Strategies must permeate the organization from the highest to the lowest levels

Especially true in large organizations, we have observed Chinese Whispers firsthand. In order to help better understand this phenomena, we developed a model for large organizations, which clearly illustrates the disconnect between the organizational strategy and specific IT projects. As part of this work, we learned that a specific organization maintained a corporate IT group numbering several hundred very capable and talented individuals who collectively worked on dozens of projects designed to help the organization achieve its strategic objectives.

After coordinating with various experts across the organization, our conclusion was simple: while the organization had a thoughtful and unambiguous strategy, there was no communication plan to assure clear dissemination across the organization. Thus, organizational units became aware of the plan in a manner like Chinese Whispers. And just like the game, the message became distorted as each organizational component shared it with the next. For example, the IT organization received the strategy from its corporate leadership and shared it with its IT divisions. The divisions, in turn, shared their understanding of the message with its IT groups, and then the IT groups shared their understanding with individual IT projects team. By the time the IT projects received the message, the organizational strategy was barely recognizable from the original plan, with each organizational component having a slightly different understanding of the plan (Figure 4.12).

This is not an isolated incident. Sadly, this tendency is common among many organizations, and we have noted this is particularly problematic for IT organizations where, despite the best intentions, they fail to align IT work with the organizational strategy.

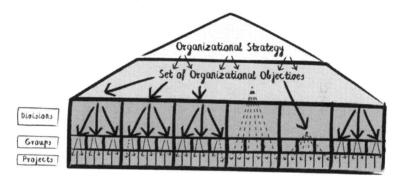

Figure 4.12 Strategies describe why organizations are doing things (communicating that strategy has not been easy)

Confronted with this kind of situation, one could reasonably ask: how does an organization maintain a strategic focus across the dozens of IT projects? The answer, of course, is that it does not. It is virtually impossible for large organizations to ensure all their projects (IT or otherwise) remain focused on supporting organizational strategy. Yet this leads us to ask ourselves another strategic question: if a project is not focused on supporting specific strategic objectives, what are the IT projects trying to accomplish and why is the organization committing resources to that work?

In the absence of a clearly communicated strategy, the bulk of the work goes on anyway, as supporting the business processes is much of what IT does (e.g., operational systems must be maintained or upgraded). So, it is new projects, major redesign or transformative programs that should be the focus of the data strategy moving forward. If left unattended, this can present a very expensive proposition for the organization. We return to this topic in a later chapter where we will discuss how to compose a data strategy and share it with the stakeholders.

MATURING DATA STRATEGY ITERATIONS

As organizations iterate their data strategy, the plan aligns more closely with the business strategy. The data strategy identifies key stakeholder functions and programs that must be aligned with one another and the business strategy. The organization slowly and painstakingly defines, organizes, funds, governs and introduces new, data-centric practices into operational elements across the organization. And as we have said, over time, the data strategy becomes the blueprint or plan, articulating how the organization will evaluate, define, plan, measure and implement new and improved data management capabilities and programs.

It for people to recognize that, at this point in the process, organizational participants will likely have no experience working in this way. It will be alien to them. It will feel uncomfortable, and some of them will likely reject what is happening. To avoid regressing, we recommend organizations start with simple tasks like setting the data strategy scope and identifying key deliverables. From there, organizations should gradually increase complexity and, with time, organizations will become more familiar with many of the concepts data-centric thinking provides. Remember: first crawl. Then walk. Then run. That is how you will be successful.

A very useful framework can be found in the DMM. It can help organizations evaluate foundational data management capabilities, which are prerequisites to more advanced data capabilities, such as data mining, MDM, data warehousing and others. The DMM model provides a framework for organizations to use when assessing the organization's ability to develop improved data management practices around the core disciplines of data: data management strategy, data quality, data governance, data platform and architecture, and data operations.

Each practice area is objectively evaluated against publicly articulated standards. The DMM framework can be used to help practitioners and executives understand what has been accomplished and what still needs to be done. This permits organizations to see where they are and to make plans for improving the current situation as they strive for world class data management practices. The first table presents the five-foundational data management practice areas and their definitions (Brackett & Mosley, 2010).

Data Management Practice Area	Definition
Data Management Strategy	managing data coherently as an organizational asset
Data Quality	maintaining fit-for-purpose data efficiently and effectively
Data Governance	managing data assets professionally
Data Platform/Architecture	using appropriate tools
Data Operations	using effective processes

The second table shows the five-level score applied to each practice area and, more importantly, to each sub-area comprising the practice area. In keeping with Sanek's weakest link theory, the organization's overall data maturity level is as strong as its weakest link. For example, if an organization has no data governance in place, it really does not matter how good its data operations are—the organization will only be as strong as its weakest link. This is analogous to getting a "D" in high school and being forever labeled a D-student.

DMM Levels	Description
1-Performed	Processes are performed ad hoc, primarily at the project level. Processes are typically not applied across business areas. Process discipline is primarily reactive; for example, data quality processes emphasize repair over prevention. Foundational improvements may exist, but improvements are not yet extended within the organization or maintained.
2–Managed	Processes are planned and executed in accordance with policy; employ skilled people with adequate resources to produce controlled outputs; involve relevant stakeholders; are monitored and controlled and evaluated for adherence to the defined process.
3–Defined	Set of standard processes is employed and consistently followed. Processes to meet specific needs are tailored from the set of standard processes according to the organization's guidelines.
4–Measured	Process metrics have been defined and are used for data management. These include management of variance, prediction and analysis using statistical and other quantitative techniques. Process performance is managed across the life of the process.
5–Optimized	Process performance is optimized through applying Level 4 analysis for target identification of improvement opportunities. Best practices are shared with peers and industry.

The DMM framework allows organizations to objectively measure progress relative to discrete data management functions and abilities. For example, Figure 4.13 reflects an airline about which management gained valuable insight as to how the organization was poorly managing and leveraging its data assets.

Using the DMM model, the organization understood its strengths and weaknesses and because the company scored low in each of the targeted area, the organization was able to make calculated, measured investments in its data strategy, data governance and data operations.

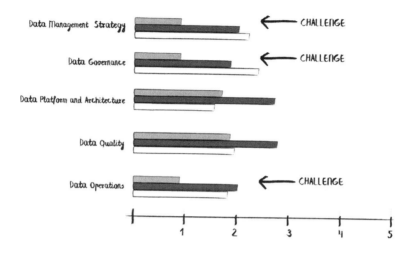

Figure 4.13 Objective DMM results for an airline client, comparison with their competition and with overall comparisons

Equally important, executives realized they were trailing the competition and could use its low scores as impetus and incentive to improve its data management capabilities, thereby raising the organization's overall data maturity. The organization could also successfully leverage data in support of its business strategy. To that end, the airline could make targeted investments in weak areas before making investments in other, stronger areas like platform, architecture and quality.

Using the DMM model to guide data strategy choices has helped many organizations rapidly achieve strategic results with their data. This is particularly important at the beginning of transformative work when the breadth of data management activities seems daunting, top-down efforts are difficult to scope and a practical, rational way forward has not yet presented itself.

References

Aiken, P., Gillenson, M., Zhang, X., & Rafner, D. (2013). Data management and data administration: Assessing 25 years of practice. *Innovations in Database Design, Web Applications and Information Systems Management* (pp. 289-309). IGI Global.

Applications Executive Council, Applications Budget, Spend and Performance Benchmarks: 2005 Member Survey Results, Washington D.C.: Corporate Executive Board 2006, p. 23.

Bonnet, P. (2013). *Enterprise Data Governance.* John Wiley & Sons.

Brackett, M. & Mosley, M. (2010). *The DAMA guide to the data management body of knowledge (DAMA-DMBOK guide).* Bradley Beach, NJ: Technics Publications.

Carnegie Mellon University. (2014). *Introduction to DMM Concepts* (pp. 1–118).

Dettmer, H. W. (1997). *Goldratt's Theory of Constraints: A Systems Approach to Continuous Improvement.* ASQ Quality Press.

Goldratt, E. M. & Cox, J. (2016). *The Goal: A Process of Ongoing Improvement.* Routledge.

Ferraiolo, D., Chandramouli, R., Kuhn, R., & Hu, V. (2016, March). Extensible access control markup language (XACML) and next generation access control (NGAC). In *Proceedings of the 2016 ACM International Workshop on Attribute Based Access Control* (pp. 13-24). ACM.

Goldratt, E. M. (1990). *Theory of Constraints.* Croton-on-Hudson: North River.

Griffin, A. & Hauser, J. R. *The voice of customer. Marketing Science* 12, (1993), 1–27.

Grundy, T. (2012). *Demystifying Strategy: How to Become a Strategic Thinker.* London, GBR: Kogan Page Ltd.

Grünig, R. & Kühn, R. (2015). *The Strategy Planning Process.* Berlin, Heidelberg: Springer.

Hill, C. & Jones, G. (2011). *Essentials of Strategic Management.* Cengage Learning.

Jin, X., Krishnan, R. & Sandhu, R. (2012, September). *A role-based administration model for attributes.* In *Proceedings of the First International Workshop on Secure and Resilient Architectures and Systems* (pp. 7-12). ACM.

Johnson, G., Scholes, K. & Whittington, R. (2008). *Exploring corporate strategy: Text and cases.* Pearson Education.

Johnson, G., Scholes, K. & Whittington, R. (2011). *Exploring Corporate Strategy* (Eighth Edition, pp. 1–659).

Jugulum, R. (2014). *Competing with High Quality Data.* Hoboken, NJ, USA: John Wiley & Sons. http://doi.org/10.1002/9781118840962.

Khatri, V. & Brown, C. V. (2010). *Designing data governance. Communications of the ACM,* 53(1), 148-152.

Laney, D., Faria, M. & Duncan, A. D. (2015). *Seven Steps to Monetizing Your Information Assets.* Gartner, 1–13.

Lynch, R. L. (2003). *Corporate Strategy.* Financial Times/Prentice Hall.

Marcionini, G., Lee, C. A. & Bowden, H. (2012). *Curating for Quality* (pp. 1–119).

Marx, G. (2006). *Future-Focused Leadership.* ASCD.

Mead, C. N. (2006). *Data interchange standards in healthcare it-computable semantic interoperability: Now possible but still difficult. Do we really need a better mousetrap? Journal of Healthcare Information Management,* 20(1), 71.

National Information Standards Organization (NISO). (2004). *Understanding Metadata.*

Moss, L. T. (2007). *Data Strategy* (pp. 1–3). EIM Insitute.org.

Nichols, K. (2015). *Enterprise Content Strategy.* XML Press.

Olson, J. E. (2003). *Data quality: the accuracy dimension.* Morgan Kaufmann.

Pitt, S. A. (2014). *Internal Audit Quality* (pp. 1–399).

Piwowar, H. A., Day, R. S. & Fridsma, D. B. (2007). *Sharing detailed research data is associated with increased citation rate. PloS one,* 2(3), e308.

Project Management Institute (PMI). (2013). *A Guide to the Project Management Body of Knowledge* (PMBOK© Guide), Fifth Edition.

Project Management Institute (PMI). (2016). *PMI Lexicon of Project Management Terms* (pp. 1–20).

Project Management Institute (PMI). (2012). *The Standard for Program Management* (pp. 1–187).

Smallwood, R. F. (2014). *Information Governance for Business Documents and Records.* (pp. 464–195b). John Wiley & Sons.

Rotondi, D. & Piccione, S. (2012, February). *Managing access control for things: a capability based approach.* In *Proceedings of the 7th International Conference on Body Area Networks* (pp. 263-268). ICST (Institute for Computer Sciences, Social-Informatics and Telecommunications Engineering).

Sacks, J. (2012, May 17). *The Limits of Secularism and the Search For Meaning.* Retrieved from http://ab.co/2mclZmw.

Singh, G., Bharathi, S., Chervenak, A., Deelman, E. et al. (2003). *A metadata catalog service for data intensive applications.* In *Proceedings of the ACM/IEEE SC2003 Conference on High Performance Networking and Computing.* (Phoenix, AZ, 2003).

Smallwood, R. F. (2014). *Information Governance,* 1–462.

Techt, U. (2014). *Goldratt and the Theory of Constraints: The Quantum Leap in Management.* Columbia University Press.

Thompson, A. A., Gamble, J. E., Strickland, A. J., III & Peteraf, M. A. (2012). *Crafting and Executing Strategy.* New York: McGraw-Hill/Irwin.

CHAPTER 5
Data Strategy at Work

Imagine. You bear ultimate accountability for the success—or failure—of your enterprise. Whether Chief Executive Officer, Chairman of the Board, President, Joint Chief of Staff, Proprietor or head of any business or government. Consider: the best decisions are made when based on the best facts. Data represents facts, either as standalone values or the sum of combinatorial manipulation.

Having described phases I and II data strategy activities above, Chapter 5 presents examples of **why and how** to develop a data strategy. Before discussing these examples, however, three short, intertwined news stories demonstrate the hidden costs of ignoring the value of organizational data.

Each deals with executives and organizations that did not value data as organizational assets and, consequently, manipulated data without a data strategy. Each failure led to some of the worst data losses in recent history and, taken together, represent glaring threat to US national security. You may have heard of them.

RIPPED FROM THE HEADLINES

What common thread connects Target, the Federal Office of Personnel Management (OPM) and Ashley Madison? Data breaches! Together, these stories clearly demonstrate the combinatorial value of data and how it can be used to deliver superior goods and services—or as a weapon against the United

States and national security. The following examines what happened to each organization's data.

TARGET: WHAT THE COMPANY KNOWS ABOUT YOU

HEADLINE!
Target Shareholders Should Oust Directors Says ISS

Shoppers pay little attention to data collection when they go shopping and, generally, are unaware of the amount of data being collected about them (Ziobro & Lublin, 2014). Nor do they necessarily understand the relative value of their data— *especially when combined with other data.*

In today's networked world, almost everything people do transfers data from one device to another. Companies routinely collect information about people, their likes and dislikes and their overall buying habits in order to sell goods and services more effectively and more efficiently.

Target is a company that knows a lot about people. Conceptually, it assigns every customer a guest identification number, a unique number that is connected to a credit card account, a name or an e-mail address and any other information the customer shares (Hill, 2012). With this information, Target can correlate each person's purchase history, demographics and other collected information, including purchases from other sources (See Figure 5.1).

Many heard about the breach of Target's information system in 2013. Hackers stole Target data and sold it on the black market. More than one hundred million shoppers were affected. Ergo, the headline.

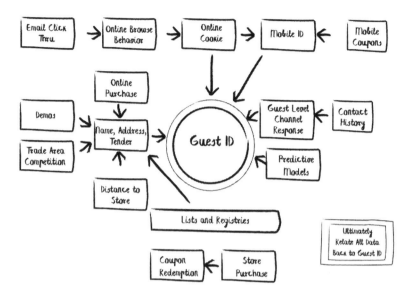

Figure 5.1 Data collection gets complete picture of guest

Target collects other information about its customers as well. Here's a sample.

- age
- cars owned
- recent moves
- ethnicity
- declared bankruptcy
- where you went to school
- political affiliations

- estimated salary
- where you live
- marital status
- credit cards
- job history
- online interests
- charitable contributions
- visited websites

- work commute
- sexual preference
- magazines read when house hunting
- preferred foods and drinks

Target analysts examined historical buying data for all women who participated in Target's baby registries. They ran countless tests and analyzed the data, and eventually patterns emerged.

Analysis results revealed that some pregnant women were purchasing large quantities of unscented lotion at the beginning of their second trimesters. Another observation revealed that, when women were about 20 weeks into pregnancy, they began purchasing vitamin supplements such as calcium, magnesium and zinc. The team also derived that those women bought lots of scent-free soap and extra-large bags of cotton balls, hand sanitizers and washcloths. Together, the purchases signaled that these women could be getting close to their delivery dates.

Analysts combed through the data and identified 25 different products which were designated as "pregnancy prediction" factors and assigned a scoring value. The analysis got better with time, and Target was finally able to estimate a baby's due date within a two-week window (Figure 5.2). With this information about pregnant women, Target was able to send mothers-to-be targeted advertising and coupons at specific points during their pregnancies.

Figure 5.2 Analytics to predict pregnancy in female customers

One day, an angry father near Minneapolis went into Target and demanded to speak with the store manager (Duhigg, 2012). He complained that his teenage daughter had received coupons for baby products in the mail. He added that his daughter was only in high school and too young to receive these kinds of materials. He then accused Target of encouraging teenage pregnancy.

The manager checked the man's claim and found that the man was right. Target's marketing materials were addressed to the man's daughter, and the advertisements showed maternity clothing, nursery furniture and pictures of smiling babies. The manager apologized and, a few days later, called the man to follow up. Imagine the manager's surprise when hearing the father's response: he had talked with his daughter about the mailer and had learned that she was, indeed, pregnant.

OPM: GOVERNMENT FAILS TO SECURE PERSONAL DATA

HEADLINE!
Jeopardizing Our National Security for More than a Generation

On June 17, 2014, the United States Investigation Service (USIS) disclosed that the Office of Personnel Management (OPM) had been breached at some time the previous March and that infiltrators had stolen personal information of more than 25 thousand federal workers and contractors (Chafetz et al, 2016); see Figure 5.3.

Figure 5.3 China hacks Office of Personnel Management and acquires information describing US government employees

Though the OPM was stunned, the organization took immediate action to sever its relationship with the contractors who were responsible for managing OPM computers. Later, Director of National Intelligence (ODNI) James Clapper confirmed that China was the lead suspect behind the OPM breach (Paletta, 2015).

While the *New York Times* reported the incident to the American people, OPM took quick action to notify its employees, informing them of the intrusion and advising federal workers to stay vigilant with regard to their personal information and any computer threats. Meanwhile, other news services reported that the break-in had all the earmarks of a state-sponsored attack. A short time later, the Federal Bureau of Investigation (FBI) started an investigation into the incident.

Federal investigators found that a government contractor, KeyPoint Government Solutions, had been hacked and that as many as 390 thousand Department of Homeland Security (DHS) employees, contractors and job applicants at other federal agencies might have had their private data compromised. US officials revealed the breach to the public in June 2015, and OPM began sending out notifications to more than 4 million current and former federal employees and contractors warning them that their personal data had been compromised. By July 2015, the FBI estimated that nearly 19.7 million people—many times the original estimate—had been affected by the OPM breach. Included in this total were more than 6 million fingerprints (Cluley, 2016).

The OPM also lost specific items of interest "cleared persons" had voluntarily disclosed to the Federal Government with the understanding that these disclosures would remain confidential. Unlike the specific behavioral and financial characteristics obtained from the Target data, OPM data contained information exclusively disclosed to the government when employees, contractors or others with need applied for clearances. When individuals apply for positions of trust, they are asked to explicitly list past transgressions of many types so these can be verified and, most importantly, not used to blackmail the applicants. Applicants provided this information to the government under conditions of trust, believing that this information was never going to see the light of day. The compromise was far-reaching: not only did the OPM lose personal information about federal employees and contractors, but it also lost personal information about their spouses, partners and other relatives.

Sadly, this specific breach occurred because unqualified officials put the private information of millions of Americans online and unnecessarily at risk. Officials who made decisions to put this data online were later deemed unqualified to make these decisions (Chaffetz, Meadows, & Hurd, 2016). OPM leadership did not possess the KSAs to judge decisions of this type. As has been seen many times, these decision-makers did not know what they did not know (Krebs, 2016).

Armed with this data, hackers could combine Target and OPM data to identify specific habits of individuals possessing security clearances. Furthermore, hackers have fingerprint data for millions of Americans that can correlate to other highly sensitive information that applicants provided the OPM.

ASHLEY MADISON: NOT KEEPING SECRETS

HEADLINE!

Ashley Madison Attackers
Threaten to Leak Extramarital Affair Data

Ashley Madison advertised its tagline: "Life is short—have an affair." This suggestion was evidently popular with millions who created individual accounts with the site. But, when news that Ashley Madison had been hacked broke in July 2015, few recognized the significance (Thomsen, 2015). What could be important about the compromise of an adult dating site? According to the news reports, the Ashley Madison web site was hacked and the company lost control of records representing tens of millions of customers' personal, biographic information.

Hackers posted the stolen information to the Internet and the information became available to anyone wishing to inspect it (Dreyfuss, 2015). Unfortunately, many Ashley Madison users never considered either the possibility—or consequences—of their data leaving the company's systems, and they never bothered to disguise their true identities. Ashley Madison users who did not use aliases became subject to extra scrutiny by those in possession of the data. This critical mistake resulted in devastating outcomes for people whose personal data was exposed.

Hackers are now using Ashley Madison data as part of several Internet "marketing" activities. Among the many whose Ashley Madison data was exposed are:

- Josh Duggar, media personality whose exposure led to public humiliation and cancellation of the family's reality TV show (Remling, 2015);

- federal employees, 44 users from whitehouse.gov and thousands of military and government e-mails;

- the Catholic Church, more than 200 e-mail addresses of staff of the Catholic Church (Staff Reporter, 2015); and

- Canadian citizens, one-fifth of the population of Quebec, earning it the title of the "most infidelity-friendly city" in Canada (Armstrong, 2015).

THE COMBINATORIAL VALUE OF THIS DATA

Taken together, the combined effect of the Target, OPM and Ashley Madison breaches might constitute the biggest threat to national security in recent years (Mascarenhas, 2016).

Manipulating the three datasets into facts, one could identify Target customers who held security clearances and who were active on Ashley Madison. It is not a stretch to imagine how hackers might use this information to assess, contact and blackmail Americans into betraying the United States. The irony? The simplicity required to make it happen.

First, simply identify all individuals who registered at Ashley Madison using their government (.gov) or military (.mil) email addresses. Then, combine this list with OPM data, resulting in the identification of people who hold positions of trust within the US Government. Finally, analysis of their habits from the Target customer database to determine anomalies might lead to candidate blackmail targets. Together, this information could be used to blackmail individuals in sensitive positions. In the end, the government's title of the final report says it all: *The OPM Data Breach: How the Government Jeopardized Our National Security for More than a Generation* (Chaffetz, Meadows, & Hurd, 2016); see link at *f. 13.*

BigOrganization Develops Its Data Strategy

So, what's the solution? Better data management—which begins with improvement or implementation of tight data strategy, one tied directly to an organization's strategy. This section presents a case study illustrating how a large, well-known organization ("BigOrganization") committed to overcoming years of laxity and applied data strategy principles within its organization. (Casey, 2016.)

BACKGROUND

BigOrganization, a high-profile organization operating in the financial sector, uses data to meet its most basic business objectives. At the time, the organization's data was siloed and managed by workers who had competing organizational responsibilities and priorities. Consequently, BigOrganization struggled to perform routine work and became consumed by an *ever-growing amount of data* generated by the organization.

Compounding matters, the organization struggled to keep pace with the global financial marketplace. For example, BigOrganization *lacked standards to facilitate data interchange and integration*, and the organization struggled with *lack of data consistency* when advising senior decision-makers. Taken together, performing routine work at BigOrganization became time-consuming, expensive and mired in bureaucracy.

Further, the organization lacked the data management discipline that would allow the organization to respond to changing economic conditions around the globe. For example, BigOrganization had no formal data governance, data architecture or data quality initiatives. Compounding matters, BigOrganization, like most organizations, performed data management well at the workgroup level but saw no real need for improving its data practice, becoming data-centric or implementing a data strategy at the enterprise level. Even though data was foundational to all its work, BigOrganization did not recognize and respect data as an asset, that is, something of value that needed to be managed and controlled.

After some time and at considerable expense, however, BigOrganization's leadership was convinced it needed a plan. It needed to set a compass bearing to help the organization prepare to be data-driven. BigOrganization needed a data strategy to guide and improve:

- the quality of its data assets;

- the ability of its knowledge workers to use data assets productively; and

- its knowledge workers' collective ability to use these data assets productively in support of the organizational strategy.

[NOTE: For this example, specific call-outs at the end of each subsection have been included to detail specific key success factors.]

Because the environment was rapidly changing, corporate leaders (who believed that troubling times were ahead if the organization did not develop and follow a data strategy) established a data strategy team. Among the many participants were members of the corporation's data governance council, a hand-picked group of leaders whose charter was to focus exclusively on data strategy. The data workgroup leveraged the enterprise data vision, goals and objectives, and the organization was more open to accepting data strategy introduction and implementation.

One of the company's data strategy themes conveyed a sense of urgency to its audience. The data strategy team took a broad view of the problem space and included P3T implications and metrics as it evaluated plans and a data roadmap. In the end, the data strategy team met its desired goal to have the plan ready for the company's budget planning cycle and, much to the surprise of team members, nearly every request received funding in the first year.

INITIATING THE STRATEGIC PLANNING PROCESS

Overcoming the Phase I data strategy critical success factors took an entire year. During the next calendar year, BigOrganization addressed Phase II: data as a tenet of the organization's strategic plan. The EDE initiated the effort with a workshop dedicated to delivering a preliminary understanding of organizational data assets and strategic uses. Members of BigOrganization's data governance council were among the participants. The council immediately began defining the vision, goals and objectives for the strategic plan. After working for several weeks, the following operating procedures were adopted:

- focus on the enterprise during planning sessions;
- consult with each member's business unit for input and guidance throughout the planning process; and
- communicate progress within each business unit; and
- advocate for enterprise solutions within each business unit.

While the council worked on the organization's strategic plan, the EDE, with confirmation from other BigOrganization executives and the data governance council, began work to align the data strategy with the organizational strategy. Using output from business processes, the EDE translated business goals and objectives into data strategy goals and objectives. This collaboration helped to manage expectations and secure buy-in from senior officials from the onset.

Afterward, because the data workgroup leveraged the enterprise data vision, goals and objectives, the organization was more open to accepting the data strategy work. This, in turn, helped the EDE jump-start follow-up work while saving time and money. Because senior leaders understood how each iteration of the data strategy would translate their organizational goals and objectives, the EDE secured support from the onset. Without having aligned the data strategy to the organizational strategy, the EDE would have been compelled to spend considerable time and resources explaining the plan and securing the support of senior leaders.

Key Success Factors

- Setting the organization on a common course.
- Securing buy-in from all stakeholders.
- Achieving sustainability throughout the entire effort.
- Receiving input from all stakeholders.

PLANNING THE WORK

A key activity of the planning process is to determine who should participate and in what capacity. To that end, the EDE considered answers to the following questions.

- What sort of process would the data strategy development follow?
- How should activities be gated?
- Who are key stakeholders and participants?
- How would communications occur and with whom?
- What project deadlines, milestones and deliverables should be established?

As part of this activity, the EDE organized work using short iterations and routine deliverables to stakeholders. A key lesson learned during the exercise was that many people in the organization were not familiar with Agile process management (Smartsheet, 2017). (Agile is addressed in more detail in chapter 6.) Consequently, team members were surprised when they received partially completed work products in quick succession. This style of work proved challenging in several other respects, chief among them the fact that the organization had a culture that recognized and rewarded work products that were detailed, encompassing and time-consuming. Despite this key difference, the workforce begrudgingly accepted the idea, and the members followed Agile practices.

Because the EDE ensured that the data council was composed of key stakeholders from the organization's strategy planning group, the group could quickly map the two planning documents, thus ensuring that the data strategy was aligned to the organization's strategic plan. Additionally, the group met for more than two years and established a level of maturity and expertise relative to key strategic challenges that the organization faced. A primary factor of the group's success was the iterative process that the team followed (see Figure 5.4).

Figure 5.4 Developing the data strategy iterates over key steps

At the same time, the EDE employed contractors to canvas the organization and conduct interviews, and contractors helped facilitate meetings and develop data strategy documentation. Recognizing that the organization was not mature relative to data and development of a data strategy, the team decided to make certain that the organization understood the plan. To this end, the EDE developed an accompanying communications plan which contained key messages and concepts about the developing data strategy. The communications plan aided the team with delivery of information to the workforce, stakeholders and leaders on a predictable and regular basis.

While this was happening, the team decided to synchronize delivery of the data strategy to coincide with the organization's annual budget cycle, thereby allotting enough time to communicate its work to BigOrganization's executive committee. Key to this was the idea that linking the data strategy to the budget cycle would most likely ensure that work described in the plan would receive funding when the data strategy was complete. If that failed, the team risked completing the strategy and having no funding to realize its goals and objectives. Following this path, the team developed, coordinated and funded the data strategy—in **less than six months**.

Finally, the team decided it would render the data strategy as a presentation (i.e., slide format) as opposed to a more traditionally used document format. As a result, the team was most efficient and effective in its communication of the plan to executives using a storytelling format. The data strategy team recognized that executives are routinely overcommitted and that sharing the data strategy in presentation format made it easier, and more timely, for the executives to understand the plan and approve it. Specifically, using slides helped the team effectively communicate complex concepts in an easy-to-understand manner, saving time and resources at each step. After a short while, the organization quickly recognized the value of this technique, and everyone in the organization began to use the same technique in other areas.

Key Success Factors

- Defining a repeatable business process for work.
- Establishing success criteria.

- Level setting of expectations among stakeholders.

- Establishing a common understanding of how the planning process works.

DEVELOPING THE STRATEGY

As the team began developing the organization's data strategy, it leveraged previous work that the enterprise strategic planning group had completed. For example, the data strategy team had direct access to the vision, goals and objectives associated with the organization's strategic plan. Because the organizational strategy was already approved, the data strategy team immediately aligned and integrated that work with the organization's data strategy.

The data strategy team was already familiar with gaps existing across the organization because it had previously spent a year working on a data management capabilities assessment. Using the assessment report, team members met with stakeholders, gathered additional information, produced updated materials and made sure to include regulatory and financial compliance information.

For instance, the team included information regarding the state of data and technology initiatives, as well as industry forecasts and best practices. Numerous focus groups were interviewed to highlight areas of opportunity and challenges with respect to BigOrganization's data, its management and its control. Ultimately, the interviews facilitated the team's development of user stories to better describe the desired outcome. On a practical level, the data strategy team met with stakeholders three times over 60 days to identify initiatives necessary to achieve five strategic objectives identified by the team.

Additionally as part of this process, the team, taking into account P3T and metrics that were needed to support its success, identified a statement of business value and KPIs for each objective. As discussed in Chapter 4, the team established a work rhythm and followed an iterative development process that addressed each component of a data strategy, including alignment with the organization's vision, goals, objectives and supporting strategies and initiatives (see Figure 5.5).

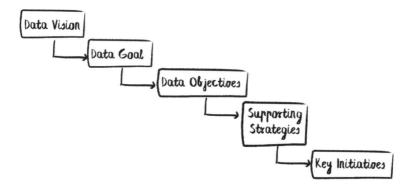

Figure 5.5 BigOrganization's deliberate process to develop its data strategy

Key Success Factors

- Ensuring the team is focused on the data strategy.

- Reducing confusion among participants.

GETTING TOGETHER FOR THE FIRST TIME

Before meeting with stakeholders, the data strategy team developed draft strategies for each objective. (The team was confident the objectives would be acceptable to stakeholders as the organization's executive leadership had already approved them.)

As the team had hoped, stakeholders were already familiar with the objectives, and the team could address issues, ideas and concerns. After discussing these items with stakeholders, the team modified the plan to reflect more well defined stakeholder needs. The data strategy team also realized that stakeholders responded more positively when the team shared draft versions with them.

The team learned that, if they discussed abstract ideas with stakeholders, conversations quickly devolved and the team made little progress toward securing executive support. However, when the team shared discrete examples of the plan, stakeholders responded positively, giving the team valuable feedback. For example, the data strategy team circulated meeting minutes, notes and talking points so stakeholders could review progress and share information with the workforce. The data strategy team also effectively used electronic approvals to help expedite decision-making and to set priorities for next steps.

Working in this iterative manner allowed the data strategy team to produce a data strategy that contained no surprises for the organization's leadership. This, in turn, also helped to ensure stakeholder support throughout the entire data strategy development process.

Key Success Factors

- Defining clear goals and objectives for planning.
- Securing explicit executive support for the plan.
- Documenting next steps.
- Reducing confusion and controversy.
- Working in a safe and trusted environment.

REPEATING SUCCESS

Building on the success of the first meeting, the data strategy team sought to achieve agreement on several key initiatives that needed to be successfully accomplished before work could begin on any other strategies.

The team took the lead and developed a draft list of initiatives for each group to discuss. As team members considered the merits of each initiative, the group added value to the effort by identifying previous omissions. Concurrently, some stakeholders revisited prior decisions, underscoring how important certain wording was to the plan. Others raised issues with respect to the volume and timing of identified programs and projects, leading the team to reorganize, rearrange and eliminate some of the strategies and initiatives originally identified.

At the close of a subsequent meeting, the team updated slides to reflect new decisions and direction and distributed the materials to stakeholders for review and approval. The last step for the data strategy team would be to prioritize all the work.

Key Success Factors

- Focusing participation on planning work.

- Opening discussion to all participants and stakeholders.

- Establishing and maintaining a creative work environment.

- Focusing the data strategy team on concept refinement.

CLOSING FOR GOLD

In the final meeting, the data strategy team focused on prioritizing all items identified in the data strategy roadmap. Consultants were sometimes used to facilitate meetings so the data strategy team could participate as an equal party. Participants set priorities for the first 12 to 18 months of the strategy. Knowing that a review of the data strategy would be needed at the end of 12 months, the team also knew there would be an opportunity to review and recalibrate the roadmap as necessary based on needs of the organization.

At the meeting, stakeholders engaged in a robust conversation about relative priorities and timing of work. The group also identified the need to coordinate with the organization's technology advisory council for some of the initiatives as there were both data and technology components involved in several of them. Also discussed were resource needs, especially human, to support the work identified in the roadmap. The data strategy team realized, too, that a headcount would be needed within both the team and business units in accordance with the then current-state data management capabilities assessment. This meant that stakeholders would not only need to advocate within their business units for the programs and projects within the data strategy, but also for increases in headcount. In a tight budget year, this work would require significant funding to succeed.

At the end of the third and last meeting, stakeholders agreed to the strategies and initiatives required to support each of the objectives identified as part of the enterprise strategic planning process. Each objective had as few as two or as many as four strategies related to each enterprise objective, and each strategy had one to three initiatives related to each strategy.

In the end, however, the consensus was that it was far too much work to be accomplished in the three-year time frame. As a best practice, it is desirable to focus on a core number of realistically achievable programs and projects. In this instance, however, several objectives had been agreed to for the enterprise strategic planning process, so some strategies and initiatives needed to be identified for each.

Key Success Factors

- Articulating clear goals and objectives.
- Achieving unified concurrence on the plan.

COMMUNICATING THE PLAN

After the work sessions, the data strategy team captured and defined several key aspects of the data strategy which stakeholders endorsed.

- Background and Overview
- Vision, Business Case, Expected Benefits and Risks of Inaction
- Data Vision, Objective, Strategies and Initiatives
- Setting Priorities for Each Iteration in the Roadmap

The data strategy team spent the last several weeks of the project fine-tuning portions of the data strategy, including risk, success enablers and budget estimates. The identification of risks to the organization early in the process provided context for the data strategy. By incorporating risks and issues into the preamble of the plan, readers could better appreciate why the organization was making certain decisions. Again, one of the data strategy themes was to convey a sense of urgency to the audience. The team also took a broad view and included P3T and metrics implications as part of each scheduled programmatic review. Most importantly, the team identified a change management framework to support organizational change readiness, training and education, sustainability, operationalization, communication and marketing. Both the data strategy team and the stakeholder group recognized the necessity for change and that it involved people at all organizational levels. Such awareness led to committed interaction of the team and stakeholder groups to build the level of awareness, understanding, buy-in and commitment necessary to support success and sustainability over the long term.

Key Success Factors

- Securing and Maintaining Stakeholder Support
- Establishing a Common Vision

REVIEWING THE WORK

Before final delivery of the data strategy, the data management team regrouped to discuss its performance and record lessons learned by collecting honest feedback from members as to what worked and what did not. The team not only collected feedback from its own membership, but it collected feedback from stakeholders as well.

Armed with these insights, the organization could make changes to the team and its processes when it was time to update the data strategy in the future. Such update was anticipated given the lack of general organizational understanding of strategy development. There were a lot of new (Phase I) concepts for the stakeholders to absorb during the process, and these occasionally ran into the reality of budget planning timelines that needed to be met.

By the time the team completed the draft version of the data strategy and presented it to the chief operating officer (COO) and the executive committee of BigOrganization, the data strategy team had addressed all major issues, leaving only minor issues to resolve. Leadership did not challenge the strategy, its goals, objective, strategies or initiatives. In the end, BigOrganization had a robust, multi-year data strategy that supported the organization's true data needs. As a byproduct, the team also created a formal data strategy development process that was adopted and documented.

Some Lessons Learned

Of note was the use of storytelling throughout the Agile process. The data strategy team quickly identified storytelling as a very effective way to communicate with executives. Knowing this, the team kept its messages short, crisp and understandable, emphasizing the importance of programs to the organization by relating user stories. Working this way helped the team introduce human elements to the strategy and showed the workforce how each person played an important role relative to the strategy and its success. Putting it simply, everyone could see themselves in the story, and they understood their roles and contributions to the organization's overall success.

Another key lesson learned was to the importance of keeping messaging short and sharp. Throughout the data strategy development process, the team deliberately cut the number of slides in half to force more efficiency with storytelling. Throughout the process, the team remained flexible and open to new ideas. Admittedly, some members would have preferred to produce details in the document but, in the end, they recognized the value of this technique, especially when executives quickly bought into the plan.

Stakeholders accepted the plan in large part because they were involved throughout the process and, as a result, they quickly reached consensus regarding the vision, goals, objectives and strategies that were needed. In the end, the team met its desired goal to deliver the plan for the budget planning cycle and, much to everyone's surprise, almost everything received funding for the first year. Today, BigOrganization is executing its data strategy with only minor modifications.

MONETIZING CONTRIBUTIONS FROM THE DATA STRATEGY

The next example describes a large logistics organization that was preparing to implement an ERP system. It conveys the manner in which the organization followed a data strategy development process that supported a hybrid decision-making approach. Based on the law of diminishing returns, this example is our first documented savings of a "person-century" (as opposed to "person-years").

Many organizations have not mastered a key step. It is important to take a holistic perspective when measuring the value accruing to the organization. This can often be a task that is "too difficult." Both authors have been on panels refuting this statement: *you can't put a price on data quality.* We disagree and include this example to illustrate how contributions from data strategies can be made concrete, a process commonly known as *monetizing* (Aiken & Billings, 2013).

These techniques were introduced during contract work for and with the Defense Information Systems Agency's (DISA) Center for Information Management in the early 1990s. At that time, DISA used the techniques to approximate various costs and benefits associated with specific information technology investment decisions. More importantly, DISA accrued substantive benefits from the focused dialog addressing concrete concepts for increasing the ability to meet organizational needs.

Illustrating the absolute basics of activity-based costing alone will expand understanding as to how to quantify business value.

However, a better understanding of costs associated with the execution of specific tasks (processes), the interactions of the tasks (process design), the automation supporting the tasks (electronic processing) and maintenance of operational models (process models) will accrue from analysis.

First, start by estimating the cost of individual participation in data improvement activities. Doing this allows one to incorporate a variety of different cost models and remedial techniques as part of each analysis. The same analyses can suggest improvements to each of the cost factors studied during analysis. Consider the scenario presented in the following four panels (Figure 5.6) from one of our favorite articulations created by Ted Rall and used by permission.

Figure 5.6 The Story of Sheena Killing an Entire Person-Day Day (© 2009 Ted Rall)

In Sheena's story, the tasks are:

- drive distractedly;

- travel through airport security; and
- slow luggage removal from an overhead bin.

This humorous example illustrates a simple accounting of Sheena's silly tasks. Sheena's impact on the time of others can be totaled and valued. (See Table 1.) This permits broader claims such as "killing a whole person-day," and we can now value the cost of this dead person-day by computing the salaries of the 520 individuals inconvenienced by Sheena. It can be valued by estimating a salary: let's say $10/hour.

Table 1: Salary Estimation

10 person-hours x $10 per hour	=	$100
12 person-hours x $10 per hour	=	$120
2 person-hours x $10 per hour	=	$20
	Total:	$240

Thus, the "Sheena" tax to society was $240 on the day in question.

Activity-based costing is just one of many measurement techniques available to evaluate data when communicating the leverage possible with advantageous data management. According to Wikipedia, activity-based costing "... assigns more indirect costs (overhead) into direct costs compared to conventional costing models." See also (Cokins, 2010) and (Kejser, Nielsen, & Thirifays, 2011).

By totaling the cost of a knowledge worker's time expended, we can approach some, but clearly not all, costs. This will permit statements such as, "At least amount *x* is being spent by this organization for task *y*." [For further information about this subject, we invite you to read the wonderful *How to Measure Anything: Finding the Value of Intangibles in Business* by Douglas W. Hubbard, ISBN: 0470539399—original edition 2007.]

We have used this basic approach for the past 20 years to calculate minimal costs associated with poor data and presented our calculations to demonstrate to management the tangible costs associated with these decisions. We have successfully combined Hubbard's and Goldratt's concepts into a workable method for evaluating and identifying primary constraints for more than a decade.

The key is to understand that, while compiling the "data" into a successful business case has not been common and therefore not easy, once you begin to repeat the process, it becomes easier.

Consider the following. A logistics organization managed over 2 million stock-keeping units (SKU) in its catalog. The challenge presented was the existence of master data maintained in clear text fields (also known as "comment" fields) in the legacy database. Prior to that time, a group of consultants succeeded in getting Oracle—a relational database management system— to act as a hierarchical database management system. Using Oracle in this fashion meant that there would be no need to change the way the organization processed its data.

Many assumed that because much of the organization's master data existed in clear text fields that the organization would have to manually extract that data. As part of their data strategy, we introduced a text mining approach that converted the non-tabular data into tabular data and verified its correctness against an evolving set of verified master SKUs.

One of the big issues involved in designing solutions such as this one is timing: when does one declare that the solution is "good enough?" Or to put it more precisely: how does one determine the point of diminishing returns? The answer: when the value from additional effort exceeds the cost of the effort. In our solution, a fixed weekly cost was one-half of the weekly salaries of two data engineers conducting the text mining, always working them in pairs.

We used one-half salary because engineers had to perform several related tasks that focused on improving the overall dataset quality, while the actual mining process took only a few hours to complete. By holding the development costs constant (one-half the weekly salaries), it was possible to discern the relative pay-offs of specific data management driven decisions.

The 18-week process is summarized in Figure 5.7.

A	B	C	D
	Unmatched items	Ignorable items	Items Matched
Week #	(% Total)	(% Total)	(% Total)
1	31.47%	1.34%	N/A
2	21.22%	6.97%	N/A
3	20.66%	7.49%	N/A
4	32.48%	11.99%	55.53%
...	...	...	...
14	9.02%	22.62%	68.36%
15	9.06%	22.62%	68.33%
16	9.53%	22.62%	67.85%
17	9.50%	22.62%	67.88%
18	7.46%	22.62%	69.62%

Figure 5.7 Establishing the point of diminishing returns

Note: Entries in brackets below refer to row and column identifiers.

The initial goal had been to achieve a 50 percent reduction in the projected workload facing the team. After the first week, exactly zero items were matched [D3], but the first week's results included identification of more than 26.8 thousand records (or 1.34 percent of the total) that could be ignored [C3] going forward. The unmatched column [B3] indicated the percentage of the SKUs with no corresponding entry in the master file (31.47 percent).

Over the next four weeks, scoring of the unmatched items remained largely unchanged [B3 to B6], but the records identified as definitively "ignorable" increased to 11.99 percent [C6] and, important from a morale perspective, matching jumped to over 55 percent [D6]. By the end of week four [ROW 6], the problem space had been reduced to two-thirds of the original challenge (55 percent [D6] + 11.99 percent [C6] = 66.99 percent). The question then changed from "Is this a good approach?" to "How long do we continue with this approach?"

Optimization was still an important consideration. To address this question, the chart was shortened, limiting the presentation of the measurement results to the last four weeks of results [rows 8-12] to show how the team easily arrived at the decision point. The revised project goal, then, was to reduce the manual effort to as little as possible within the original project budget guidelines. Weekly progress was reviewed by the teams, and accomplishments were significant.

- A decrease in unmatched items from 32 percent to 7.46 percent [B6 to B12], meaning that, in real SKU terms, of the original 2 million individual SKUs, only about 150,000 now required manual intervention. The text mining process, combined with the automated workflow, addressed 92.5 percent of the original problem space.

- An increase in the number of ignorable items from just under 11.99 percent [C6] to 22.62 percent [C12]. More than 450,000 SKUs were immediately ignorable, reducing the problem space by more than 20 percent. An increase in the items matched from 55 percent [D6] to just under 70 percent [D12], indicating a successful creation of the resulting, high-value golden master copy of the item master file.

This outcome permitted calculation of specific values such as *per SKU* and *per person-year*. The project team agreed that only incremental value could be achieved after week 18 and, thus, terminated refinement of the text mining at that point. These results were compared against the proposed manual extraction process. For the purposes of comparison, each person-year of effort was valued at $60,000, and the agreed-to total project value is shown in Figure 5.8.

It was agreed that this iteration of data strategy support had contributed a cumulative value of at least $5.5 million when using a time measure of only five minutes (the assumption on Row 2) to review and cleanse each individual data item. Of course, such a number was ludicrous, and that precise point was made during presentation of the results.

The key was the observation that, if the time required was doubled to 10 minutes per SKU, it would require 186 person-years; if the time permitted was 15 minutes, it would require 279 person-years to accomplish the task—almost three person-centuries. In our experience, very few data quality challenges require only 15 minutes to resolve. This likely pushes the savings higher still.

Time needed to review all DSDs once over the life of the project:	
DSDs	2,000,000
Average time to review and cleanse(in minutes	5 mins
Total Time (in minutes)	10,000,000

Time available per resource over s 1 year period:	
Work weeks in a year	48
Work days in a week	5
Work hours in a day	7.5
Work minutes in a day	450
totale work minutes in a year	108,000

Person years to cleanse each DSD once to migration:	
Minutes needed	10,000,000
Minutes available per year	108,000
Total person-years	92.6

Resource cost to cleanse DSD's prior to migration:	
Average salary for SME a yer (not including overhead	$60,000
Projected years required to cleanse/totla person years saved	93

TOTAL COST TO CLEANSE / TOTAL SAVINGS TO CLEANSE DSDS: $5.5 million

Figure 5.8 Proving return on investment of the strategy instantiation— a person-century of savings

BIGRETAILER EXAMPLE—REENGINEERING THE LOCATION DATA ELEMENT

This last example illustrates a specific data constraint requiring a strategic organizational data response.

BigRetailer attempted to achieve low prices for its customers. Barriers included internal constraints to processes, systems and the organization, and such things as people, policies and equipment. There may also be external constraints, for example, changing regulations or resource scarcity. A specific example includes a focus on addressing the amount of time it takes BigRetailer to issue new store numbers.

Because the amount of time BigRetailer takes to issue new store numbers could significantly and adversely affect the company's ability to generate new and increased annual revenue, BigRetailer may determine this would be a constraint worth reviewing and potentially reworking. As part of this rework, data management experts should be asking questions such as: "What, if anything, is holding the company back from issuing store numbers faster than they currently are?" Sometimes, the answers to these kinds of questions are obvious. For example, system bottlenecks can be easy to identify. At other times, however, constraints may be more subtle. For example, business analysts may generate incorrect performance metrics. Problems such as this would most likely go unnoticed until an outside actor inspected or verified BigRetailer's performance statistics as part of an outside audit or inspection. Additionally, one needs to carefully identify true constraints and not symptoms or reflections of the true, underlying problems.

Suppose BigRetailer uses a three-digit identifier code for store numbers called *store-id*. This gives them a potential for 999 stores. They had several hundred stores as of 2016. In this hypothetical example, BigRetailer has misused its "primary key" field, *store-id*. By misused, we mean it was used for things other than store, such as providing a unique identifier to locations like vendor kiosks outside of existing BigRetailer stores. As a result, the existing code *store-id* can be used to determine kiosk locations as well as store locations. Adding just one kiosk at each BigRetailer store would use up all 999 existing unique *store-ids* long before BigRetailer had achieved 1,000 store locations.

The situation facing BigRetailer might be described as a major, systemic data issue whereby a key, fixed-length identifying variable was overflowing and required re-specification of one of BigRetailer's most fundamental business objects: *location*. Reengineering *location* involved identifying, managing and controlling the evolution of a widely implemented, organizationally common variable: a "master" data item.

[Note: an enterprise data model would aid this process, but BigRetailer had not invested in this type of programmatic effort.]

The effect of this problem had far-reaching consequences: if BigRetailer could not add new store numbers to its various information systems, then it could not account for revenue coming from the new stores in its overall financial performance. You can be certain shareholders are concerned whenever an "IT" challenge prevents the company from adding revenue and increasing perceived share valuation. There are, of course, more practical constraints imposed by the lack of ability to add new *store-ids*. These include: inability to accrue sales to the new stores, inability to ship inventory to the new stores, inability to assign personnel to the new stores, *et cetera*. Literally, death by a thousand cuts.

Investigation by BigRetailer IT hypothetically indicated that the three-digit *store-id* occurred in hundreds of BigRetailer IT systems and would have to be remediated in each of these hundreds of systems in order to eliminate the constraint. As referenced above, the cost of this issue had been estimated to vastly exceed the amount spent on the Year 2000 (Y2K) fix. The proposed redress threatened to consume a large portion of future IT budgets and, in turn, resources needed for new business-driven initiatives. The business side articulated constant frustration with IT's inability to deliver satisfactory plans for resolving this issue.

An inability to account for new store sales seems a reasonably important constraint to BigRetailer's organizational strategy of competitive pricing. The data strategy thus might be focused on eliminating the *store-id* constraint.

Solution alternatives include adding an attribute to the *store-id* indicating whether the location is a store or a kiosk or removing all non-store *store-ids* and reallocating all the accumulated data to the new identifiers. A further complication then was that all fields were numeric, removing the option of incorporating letters with numbers in the field. (Lack of a similar technical restriction permitted a solution incorporating letters into reservation numbers that airlines implemented.)

In order to address this constraint, BigRetailer must do one of two things: (1) increase the size of the *store-id* field across all of its hundreds of IT systems, or (2) eliminate all non-store uses of this field (i.e., remove all kiosks from using *store-id* as a primary identifier). Neither is a pretty alternative. Fixing or adding a new identifier (for example, *location-id*) to all hundreds of existing IT systems is a non-trivial challenge and had been forecast to cost more than correcting the Y2K bug. Yet exploiting this system constraint requires one or the other solution—there are no other alternatives.

Given that either solution is a complex, intricate, invasive process involving hundreds of modifications to existing IT systems, it really doesn't matter which one BigRetailer hypothetically selects. The point is that, for the duration of the data strategy sprint, everything else is subordinate to addressing the *store-id* challenge in order to report increased revenue to shareholders as soon as possible.

Looking at a discrete iteration within the strategy development process, BigOrganization realized that all IT projects must include a *"store-id"* remediation component. Additionally, all business re-engineering projects required explicit conformance with the new *store-id* standard, and all capital investments in hardware, software or process improvement must use the new corporate *store-id* standard.

This is a mandatory step. If not implemented forcefully, existing projects will tend to revert to previous behavior and standards (or lack thereof).

In this example, BigRetailer would elevate this constraint to the priority data strategy for the next cycle. All other data and many IT priorities would be subordinated to the task of addressing the *store-id* problem. Upon seeing the problem, company representatives were aghast that the team had overlooked such an obvious and easily-remedied problem, especially one that had such a potentially profound effect upon the company's profitability.

Once time, cost and schedule have been established, it is appropriate to begin the next iteration. Consider the next item on the list and verify that it should still be the next in sequence.

[Note: Often, analysis in a previous cycle will make a subsequent step redundant, obsolete or trivial, so it is always a good idea to subject each iteration's focus to a critical review.]

In our example, regular sessions would be held as part of data governance to review progress and ensure another constraint had not gained sufficiency to be elevated over the *store-id* mess. Discipline is necessary to remain focused while maintaining enough objectivity to be alert to other constraints requiring elevation. When considering budget (a pattern in a stream of decisions), priority will be given to *store-id* expansion explicitly

at the expense of other requirements. The nature of strategy
follows.

- **Analysis:** result indicating need for corporate decision
  that *store-id* expansion subsumes all other data
  priorities
- **Choice:** selection of one of the two stated alternatives for
  iteration organization-wide
- **Iteration:** focus on addressing this issue until it is
  possible to determine how long it will take, how much it
  will cost and when it can be completed

Absent this last analysis, it is ridiculous to move to version N+1
of a BigRetailer's (or any organization's) data strategy because,
if you cannot anticipate how long it will take, how much it will
cost, or when it will be complete, then elevating another issue to
the strategic level is absurd.

References

Armstrong, J. (2015, July 22). *1 in 5 Ottawa residents are on Ashley Madison. What makes the city so infidelity-friendly?* Retrieved from http://bit.ly/1PqiL7z.

Chaffetz, J., Meadows, M. & Hurd, W. (2016). *The OPM Data Breach: How the government jeopardized our national security for more than a generation* (pp. 1-231, Rep.). Washington, DC: Committee on Oversight and Cluley, G. (2016, September 08). Retrieved from http://bit.ly/2mTVlDd.

Cokins, G. (2010). *Performance Management.* John Wiley and Sons.

Dreyfuss, E. (2015, August 19). *How to check if you or a loved one were exposed in the Ashley Madison hack.* Retrieved from http://bit.ly/24HlG4o.

Kejser, U. B., Nielsen, A. B. & Thirifays, A. (2011). *Cost model for digital preservation: Cost of digital migration. The International Journal of Digital Curation.* http://doi.org/10.2218/ijdc.v6i1.186.

Krebs, B. (2016, September 7). *Congressional Report Slams OPM on data breach*. Retrieved from http://bit.ly/2csCXdK.

Mascarenhas, H. (2016, November 14*). FriendFinder Networks data breach exposes over 400 million adult site accounts*. Retrieved from http://bit.ly/2mMKMkW.

Paletta, D. (2015, June 25). *U.S. Intelligence Chief James Clapper Suggests China Behind OPM Breach*. Retrieved from http://on.wsj.com/2ngn4vn.

Rall, Ted. *The Story of Sheena Killing an Entire Person-Day*. N.p.: n.p., 2009. Print

Remling, A. (2015, August 20). *'19 kids and counting' star Josh Duggar admits he was unfaithful to wife Anna after Ashley Madison leak*. Retrieved from http://bit.ly/2mTHMUq.

Report, M. S., Chaffetz, C. H., Committee on Oversight and Government Reform, & Meadows, C. H. (2017).

Smartsheet. *Comprehensive Guide to the Agile Manifesto*. Smartsheet. N.p., 01 Nov. 2016. Web. 24 Apr. 2017.

Staff Reporter. (2015, August 25). *Blogger says Vatican workers were not listed among users of Ashley Madison site*. Retrieved from http://bit.ly/1MByTUF.

Thomsen, S. (2015). Extramarital affair website Ashley Madison has been hacked and attackers are threatening to leak data online." *Business Insider, 20 July 2015. Web. 24 Apr. 2017.*

Wall Street Journal (May 28, 2014). *Target shareholders should oust directors says ISSl.*

Ziobro, P. & Lublin, J. S. (2014, May 28). *Target Shareholders Should Oust Directors Says ISS. Wall Street Journal.*

CHAPTER 6
The Data Doctrine

The following is a lofty phrase used by the European Union (EU) to indicate its highest regard for personal data (Vollmer, 2016):

The processing of personal data should be designed to serve mankind.

This statement serves as a clear and unambiguous measure against which various activities are evaluated. The reason for such a forceful declaration is that no aspect of our society is immune from poorly treated data assets, and the consequences of this are many and profound. For example, consider the societal cost of email inboxes cluttered with spam. Consider the cost to organizations having to constantly patrol their systems in search of digital garbage and questionable material. Consider the financial investments that organizations must make to stay ahead of an ever-increasing and relentless deluge of irrelevant and obstructive waste.

We added Chapter 6 after we realized that, while many were using the phrase "data-centric thinking," no one had defined it. No one had put forth a definition that others could evaluate and critique. As of this writing, there is no standard, consensus-based definition in academic or popular literature and, to that end, we offer a definition and encourage an open and honest discussion to ratify a commonly accepted definition. Additionally, this chapter builds on the groundbreaking work that the Agile software movement introduced to software development. We illustrate why Agile software practices—as beneficial as they have been—are still insufficient to restore faith in IT. In the spirit of the Agile *Manifesto*, we introduce *The Data Doctrine* as a specific set of objective practices that enable organizations to better marshal data assets in support of their organizational and data strategies. The doctrine is a broadly accepted but evolving set of principles. If adopted, these principles help organizations leverage their data and introduce data-centric thinking. Next, we review the consequences if organizations decide not to adopt data-centric thinking. The four tenets of the data doctrine are introduced. The book concludes with a short overview of Agile tenets. But first...

CONSEQUENCES OF FAILURE TO ADOPT DATA-CENTRIC THINKING

The fact that any data-centric dialog is occurring at all is encouraging. However, more needs to be done if business and those who perform its operations are to increase data literacy. Look around; you can recognize consequences of ignoring the foundational role that data plays in our organizations.

- There is inadequate or nonexistent data education at all levels, which leads to lack of appreciation by knowledge workers for the value of shared data assets. This, in turn, leads organizations to focus on easier to conceptualize efforts such as software development.

- Lack of data awareness leads organizations to ignore need for data programs and, instead, attempt to manage shared organizational data assets at the project level.

- Lack of data programs leads to increases in IT spending. Consequently, organizations expend resources on activities such as integrating and cleaning data or managing far more data than is necessary to manage strategically.

- Lack of ability to prepare for future change by implementing a flexible and adaptable organizational data architecture also unnecessarily expends resources.

- A vague focus on the ability of data assets to efficiently and effectively support organizational strategy leads to diminished organizational performance

- Voluminous amounts of unmanaged data increase the amount of complexity within an organization.

- Increasing amounts of time, efforts and risk associated with IT projects threatens budgetary bottom lines

- Inability to engineer flexibility and adaptability into architectures before production requires additional time and funding to correct adverse effects of such inability.

- Lack of ability to produce reusable data-focused work products requires duplication of effort, diminishes quality and reliability of information—and costs money.

- Increasing time spent understanding data and corresponding decreases time and cost expended for analysis.

- Lack of understanding of data assets inhibits any ability to consider (much less implement) data-focused portions of organizational strategy.

- Reduction in the certainty benefits of engineered solutions is an adverse result of not understanding organizational data assets.

- Finally—and perhaps the most egregious, the resulting increased organizational data ROT just makes everything worse.

MORE ABOUT DATA ROT

Failure to adopt data-centric thinking has led to the current state of affairs. Specifically, far too much data is of poor quality, is redundant and doesn't meet the definition of organizational asset. We mentioned earlier that this is known as data *ROT*.

Data—like many natural resources—has a lifecycle, which means data may lose its relative value at some time and become outmoded for its originally intended purpose. And now that data and the relative cost of technology are well within the bounds of affordability, it is technically simple to generate copies of data for a wide variety of individual purposes. When this happens, data grows at startling rates and in ways that organizational leaders cannot imagine.

For example, it is very easy for people to generate countless, redundant copies of data that quickly populate an organization's information technology landscape. In these cases, people briefly use the data for a task, and then their attention is re-directed to a different task. Assigned new work, people quickly forget about the data they generated, leaving it where it rests and never using it again. This kind of behavior is the force behind something called *dark data*, which is a particular kind of data ROT. Gartner defines dark data as information assets organizations collect, process and store in the course of their regular business activity but generally fail to use for other purposes (Tittel, 2016).

OBSTRUCTING DATA STRATEGY DEVELOPMENT

Today, more organizations consider strategic planning to be a task for top management. Despite great personal commitment of those in charge, results have often been unsatisfactory. Such strategies are not sufficiently based on realities and true environmental complexities to create success in a competitive environment. The following comments address some of these common impediments to developing an effective and successful data strategy.

- **No Existing Data Governance.** Organizations suffer from excessive compartmentalization, which leads to narrowly focused governance and parochial definitions that represent only a selected organizational population. The problem only worsens with the advent of big data, cloud deployment models, mobility and social data (Buytendijk, 2015).

- **Too Many Strategic Documents.** There's too much strategy documentation, and it's generally poorly-coordinated—and often contradicting. This happens especially in larger organizations where different organizational units at different strata produce different strategic documentation at different times (Grunig, 2015).

- **Overdependence on Technology.** Traditional IT leaders tend to be project-focused rather than data-focused. This typically means that conflicting data definitions are created during each project as per traditional way for projects to operate.

- **Vague Authority and Accountability.** Responsibility, answerability—and thus justification—are essential to successful execution. Because of this, organizations must ensure that roles, responsibilities and reporting lines are determined, designed, documented and delivered to staff using more "pictures" and fewer "words" to all stakeholders (Latif, 2013).

- **Lack of Planning.** In many organizations, leadership is more focused on performing day-to-day activities than planning for the future.

- **Lack of Commitment.** Leaders must be committed and remain engaged throughout the entire data strategy development process. When management fails to take interest in the formulation and iteration of strategy, other problems will quickly follow.

- **Inflated Expectations.** Managers fail to adequately estimate the training for employees to implement the strategy. Not only does this cost more and take longer, it also creates organizational tension if end users become frustrated with pursuit of assigned objectives designed to achieve strategic goals.

- **Lack of Decision-Making Protocols.** To ensure that employees take part in the planning process, introduce and implement change management methodologies so that engaged employees can both offer and receive feedback about expected outcomes.

- **Inconsistent Vocabulary.** Few organizations use a common language to describe business information or the semantics and syntax surrounding it. Instead, different, divergent and sometimes conflicting words are used throughout the organization to describe the same relevant, real world phenomena. This situation poses significant obstacles for information technology experts.

- **Alignment.** A cogent, crisp and concisely written summary of the data strategy lays the foundation for correctly positioning groups, individuals and processes across organizations.

- **Lack of Perceived Value.** Each organization inherently develops a value system that generally is reflected in its mission and the goals and objectives established to achieve it. Only when the value assigned to data reflects its significant importance will leaders avoid the risk of encountering conflict with IT efforts. (Carnegie Mellon University, 2014).

- **Lack of Effective Communications.** Promulgation is the act of formally proclaiming or declaring a new policy after its enactment. Published policies, standards and other guidelines should be readily available to members of the organization. Often this is accomplished through a centralized electronic library (Carnegie Mellon University, 2014). For example, the organization's foundational business glossary can be made available electronically to employees who, though sharing data, often use different terms or phrases to refer to the data values being shared. Centralization of this information permits one-stop-shopping for the latest version of both terms and adopted definitions.

Organizations need to ensure their data strategy is aligned to the organizational strategy before considering any software acquisition or development efforts. Moreover, well-engineered data structures are needed to support organizational strategies. Because data structure changes, it is important to carefully manage software, its code and physical definitions. As a best practice then, organizations need to ensure that data architecture is flexible and adaptable and that projects include consideration of explicit data costs as part of their operations and maintenance estimates. And finally, organizations should focus on reducing data ROT, improving quality, increasing security and expanding data reuse.

DEFINING DATA-CENTRIC THINKING: *THE DATA DOCTRINE*

If you recognized your organization somewhere in the previous lists, you will be happy to learn that there is hope. In this section, because improving software development aspects of systems development is a good and necessary step, we present a necessary supplement to the *Manifesto* as it is insufficient by itself. More is needed. Embracing *the Data Doctrine* (Aiken & Harbour, 2017) will result in more concrete, improved and important system components resulting in enhanced Agile efforts.

As a class of assets, data has not been leveraged anywhere close to its full potential to support organizational strategy because:

- data management and software development have not been separated and sequenced;

- data structures have not been stabilized before software is given access to them;

- shared data structures lack programmatic development and evaluation; and

- reusable software has been valued more than reusable data.

Most organizations have been unsuccessful at implementing an effective data strategy for one of these reasons. Moreover, data leveraging efforts have suffered because organizations do not employ *data-centric thinking*. Part of the challenge is the fact that we have had trouble correctly conceptualizing the challenge. Figure 6.1 illustrates a common description of system components which normally includes people, processes, hardware, software and data. This representation is misleading, however, in that it shows all components as being equal. This is especially not true for the relationship between software and data. Because of the increasing Vs (see again, Chapter 2), data fundamentally requires engineering-based and increasingly science-based processing.

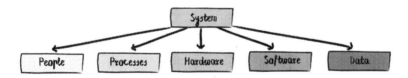

Figure 6.1 Primary system components

Google the term *data-centric thinking*, and a variety of different responses appear in your browser. As of this writing, no standard or consensus-based definition has appeared in academic or other popular literature. Therefore, we offer the following for others to review and improve.

Everyone needs to possess an objective baseline understanding of *data-centric thinking* to have a standard against which to compare observed practice. Because the educational system has been disconnected from real world data practice, data and its management have progressed slowly from an academic perspective. Resulting vagueness has led to misunderstanding both data and its role relative to projects, information technology, organizations and society, in general.

Note: We commend the "data first" approach to software development as a step in the right direction. See, for example, the discussion at http://bit.ly/2mEpHbW.

We are uncovering better ways of developing IT systems by doing it and helping others do it. Through this work, we have come to value:

- data programs preceding software projects,
- stable data structures preceding stable code,
- shared data preceding completed software, and
- reusable data preceding reusable code.

That is, while there is value in the items on the right, we value the items on the left more.

Figure 6.2 Foundational Value Assertions of The Data Doctrine

We offer *The Data Doctrine* as a plan for data-centric development of business and IT systems. We intend to maintain this discussion online with dialog dedicated to improving the overall articulation of the Doctrine. Figure 6.2 presents the primal assertions of the Doctrine. (Join the conversation by signing up at http://thedatadoctrine.com.)

Put into practice, we consider the above to be basic tenets of data-centric thinking. The doctrine uses thoughts, ideas and inspiration from numerous sources including the original *Agile*

Manifesto (Morgan, 2016). We consider *The Data Doctrine* necessary because data *programs* are inherently and substantially different from and far less successful than software (see again, Figure 6.2).

Work to produce software is generally organized as projects that have discrete beginnings and endings. These are regularly called *software projects* and are often organized into families of projects for more complicated efforts. Because data is a shared resource, data assets must be managed independent of any project, ideally as its own program. Because data is incorporated into multiple software systems, the data program must exist at a higher (horizontal) level of abstraction and maturity than software. Therefore, for organizations to effectively incorporate data assets into their organizational strategy, they must establish a separate data management program exhibiting the following four assertions.

DATA-CENTRIC PREMISE NO. 1: VALUE DATA PROGRAMS PRECEDING SOFTWARE PROJECTS

While many have promoted software reuse, the reality is that, outside of the community of open-source software, very little software gets reused. This is because if software code is to be reused, it must attain a critical mass of interest. Software code of interest to a few coders cannot sustain the notice, focus and enthusiasm required by a community of interest and is, consequently, rarely reused.

On the other hand, it is comparatively easy to define the syntax and semantics of a specific, shared data element. According to author Robert Smallword, data has been managed for millennia in books, ledgers and logs (Smallwood, 2014). Still, very few data repositories remain in operation over long periods of time. Our colleague, David Eddy, postulated that only 5 percent of enterprise-level repositories created between 1973 and 2003 are still in use, making it incredibly difficult to sustain reusable, basic and elemental data (Eddy, 2011 & 2013).

To derive the highest value from its data, organizations need to position their data as organizational assets and align them— along with other assets—with the organization's strategic objectives. When organizations do this, they increase the strategic value of their data and enable its reuse across multiple software systems versus a single system. To achieve this, organizations must deliberately guide data's reuse across multiple software projects. Putting it in programmatic terminology, this kind work is a *program*, an effort that is initiated and continues (repeats) until the organization decides it no longer needs to perform this kind of work or the organization ceases to exist.

This is illustrated in Figure 6.3 below (reproduced from Figure 3.5). An evolving data strategy results from step-wise refinement of different IT project development cycles. Several software development iterations must occur for data management activities to reach a tipping point- and contribute in support of organizational strategy.

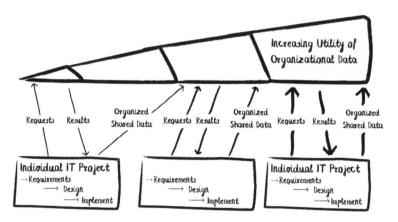

Figure 6.3 Individual IT projects make increasing use of an organization's data strategy

Over time, requests for a data strategy increase as knowledge workers and developers increase their acknowledgment and understanding of data-centric thinking and integrate that understanding into everyday activities. Similarly, as a data strategy increases in scope, it continues to become more important to knowledge workers. Each subsequent application system contributes enhanced data assets.

Evidence indicates that this re-iterative interaction between IT application systems development and data architecture and evolution is simply not being performed in most organizations. Under the application system's development paradigm, data architectures are created entirely within application system boundaries and are thus unusable by other parts of the organization. Data leveraging is prevented. To this end, it is clear that:

Data programs must precede software projects.

DATA-CENTRIC PREMISE NO. 2: VALUE STABLE DATA STRUCTURES PRECEDING STABLE CODE

As we have described, there are some fundamental flaws with the process of incorporating data development into existing software development methods. These weaknesses can be summed up in a simple phrase: "the only way existing systems can deliver effective results—given today's software guidance—is when no data sharing occurs across software projects." In today's fast-paced business environment, a tremendous amount of data gets shared, and having to wade through overly complex processes to share data only consumes more resources and impedes progress if implanted at the project level. However, if one considers the relationship between software and data, priority should be given to developing data structures before software code.

Here is an example of what has happened in typical university classrooms for many years.

As part of a capstone course in computer science, information systems and computer engineering, students are given the task of developing a database and software to access the developed database. As part of the official course instructions, students are told:

Most (80 percent) of you will misunderstand the data structure requirements you are given in this course and, as a result, you will build your databases incorrectly. You will discover this about three weeks before the end of the semester. Your mistaken understanding of the data (and therefore database) requirements will cause to you must rebuild the database to correct the data structure errors approximately three weeks before this course ends. Redefining and implementing these new data structures will cause you to have to redesign and reconstruct the entire database and all the programs you have spent the better part of the semester building. This is an entirely avoidable error, and yet most of you will make and then must correct these errors despite this warning. This will cause most of you to have to accomplish again the entire semester's coursework during the last three weeks to receive a passing grade. While we would like for you to not have to go through this painful exercise in futility, as they say, you can lead a horse to water, but you cannot make the horse drink. You have all been officially warned of this impending complication to your graduation.

The key to understanding the issues that regularly surfaced during this exercise is realizing that program access, control and flow structures are all dependent on having stable structures (i.e., syntax) in the database that multiple software programs share. Change the database and one must literally inspect and possibly change all the programs accessing the database to determine the propagation effect of the new data structures. These effects can be as simple as file access or as complex as new workflows required to service the new data structures.

A quick example may help (see Figure 6.4). Starting at the top of the left model, suppose an organization has software with a data structure that has a business rule [BR] requiring that a person can be employed as only one employee [BR1] and that each employee can only hold one position at a time [BR2]. This rule works so long as the practices comport with existing structures in the database. What routinely happens, however, is that people discover discrepancies after the software-database combination is purchased, acquired, installed and put into use. By this time, there is generally no fast, easy, cost-effective way to make changes.

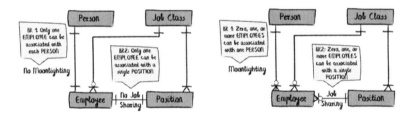

Figure 6.4 Fundamental data structure flaws force complexity into software (two design options illustrated); the (right) data model more flexibly implements user requirements

However, the rules are rarely this simple. What is more likely to happen is that organizations may implement different business rules. For example [BR3], persons can be employed as multiple employees (permitting "moonlighting") or that a position can be occupied by more than one employee (permitting "job sharing").

If the fundamental data structures do not support these scenarios, then the alternative is to implement them with software or non-automated practices. For example, if moonlighting is not allowed by "the system" or "the computer" and the organization desired it, the employee would be tagged by the system as Employee ID#1 for the first job and Employee ID#2 as the second job, and it would be someone's or some software program's responsibility to account for both of these jobs in order to properly compile tax and other reporting information annually.

A parallel set of requirements (unmet in the top section of the figure) apply to the implementation of the job-sharing data structure [BR4]. Clearly, the better approach is to have these capabilities built into the data structures instead of retrofitted in software. This is the primary reason most software vendors never change their data models once the original has shipped (Parker and Mattia, 2007).

An example of the impact that data structure changes can have on software comes from the way the organizational software performs scheduling. If job sharing is not permitted, then each EMPLOYEE has one POSITION and each POSITION is filled by exactly one EMPLOYEE [BR1]. Scheduling is accomplished when an EMPLOYEE is scheduled full time for a single POSITION (the only option). This can be done with much less information (one employee = one position) than under conditions permitting job sharing. This scheduling must be accomplished with additional coordination complexity involving an EMPLOYEE, a POSITION and a SCHEDULE, and perhaps a different instance daily depending on the granularity of the job sharing permitted.

While we understand the preference for delivering working software over documentation, the *Agile Manifesto* does not recognize the key role that organizationally shared data structures play in software projects. As you can see from the above discussion, changes to the data structure can impact every program accessing the data structures. Hence it is clear that:

Data evolution must be separated from, external to, and precede software projects.

DATA-CENTRIC PREMISE NO. 3: VALUE SHARED DATA PRECEDING COMPLETED SOFTWARE

Repeatedly reviewing project work is crucial to the development process: each iteration helps the team better understand the project's software requirements—from simple unit functionality to overall system behavior. However, as noted above, if data structures change at any point during an iteration, coding must stop until the team can address and resolve any issues related to those data structures. When software changes, there are generally fewer consequences than when shared data structures change because software is more adaptable and malleable than shared data structures. Shared data structures are foundational to every software system and, when they change, ripple effects can distress the entire system.

The *Agile Manifesto* illustrates a common and recurring issue: organizations rarely define data until it is reused, instead of defining it and treating it as something shared *before* it is used. Such afterthought creates all manner of preventable problems: the practice costs more, delivers less, takes longer and presents greater risk. One obvious example occurs when software projects expect data to have been identified, specified and documented. In programmatic terms, physical data structures must exist before any software projects can incorporate them correctly. Additionally, if organizations expect to reuse that data, they must first exercise data design principles that promote reuse over single use.

Data structures must be stabilized before the software accessing them is constructed.

DATA-CENTRIC PREMISE NO. 4: VALUE REUSABLE DATA PRECEDING REUSABLE CODE

Establishing the pedigree of data has been a longstanding problem. Underlying causes of the problem include the following, among others.

- Organizations fail to recognize the value of data.

- Organizations fail to recognize that data needs to be reused.

- Organizations fail to appreciate the value of documenting data and making it ready for reuse.

- Organizations fail to clearly define data governance, authorities and processes relative to data and its reuse.

When this sort of foundational work and documentation are produced up front—including better sets of project guardrails, common understanding of fundamental concepts and improved resource and cost estimates, other benefits accrue. Articulating and documenting data's origin, characteristics and handing procedures represent metadata management challenges discussed previously.

Organizations need to develop processes to support the collection of data provenance as well as data requirements before anyone begins to write software. Were organizations to operate in this manner, they would construct software projects based on shared, stable data structures, specifications and documentation. However, because most organizations are comfortable with technology, they rush past the inescapable fact that, if organizations do not have stable data, individual software projects will generate project-specific data and data structures. When this happens, the organization positions itself to incur measurably more cost and effort when it later tries to integrate systems and share data.

Reusable data must be valued more than reusable software.

WHY DATA HAS FARED POORLY

There are several reasons why the ability to use data assets in support of organizational strategies has suffered.

- Data management and software development have not been separated and sequenced.

- Data structures have not been stabilized before software is given access to them.

- Shared data structures lack programmatic development and evaluation.

- Reusable software has been valued more than reusable data.

Combined, these are the reasons that organizations have been unable to implement data strategies. Efforts to address the inherent situations represented have been challenged at all levels, most particularly at project, program, organizational and societal levels. Each is addressed briefly below.

SHARING DATA AMONG PROJECTS

Sharing data outside of projects has been difficult because projects tend to focus on things within project boundaries (not requiring authorization) and sharing is, by definition, crossing boundaries. Project budgets are generally used to pay for things within project boundaries. Without the benefit of an organizational data sharing program, individual projects are compelled to bear the cost of leveraging shared data on a project-by-project basis. From a cost perspective, this is analogous to asking society to inefficiently pay for police and fire departments using fees that accrue to individual users when they need these services. Data sharing is a programmatically-grounded activity based on processes that are articulated, formalized and authoritative. Until organizations realize that shared data can only be achieved through deliberate, regulated, organizationally-standardized efforts, they will determine all too late that it is not beneficial to make these investments at all.

USING INFORMATION TECHNOLOGY TO SHARE DATA

IT leadership has been focused on managing numerous, diverse activities (Aiken & Gorman, 2013). This focus has not been conducive to the implementation of data sharing programs (Aiken & Gillenson 2011). In general, IT has not managed to implement advantageous, enterprise-wide data sharing programs in most organizations. In our experience, nine out of10 organizations struggle daily with disjointed data. One in10 organizations has proven willing to make and implement robust data management capabilities.

Poor data management capabilities have been the root cause of nearly every IT failure we have studied (numbering now in the hundreds). Consider the following articulation of one organization's IT environment. Figure 6.5 shows a typical IT perspective of their world.

Of note, this illustration hardly acknowledges data at all. The images show only two veiled references to data: (1) two data centers and (2) 1,100 terabytes of data. Without knowing anything more about this organization, we can assure you that it can benefit from more data-centric thinking.

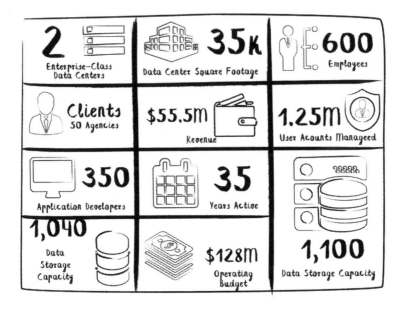

Figure 6.5 One Organization's articulation of its IT environment

SHARING DATA IN ORGANIZATIONS

Organizations cannot know what they do not know and, in many cases, organizational leadership assumes IT is responsible for sharing data. After all, many organizations maintain an official position for "Chief Information Officer," and what else would that individual do except be an excellent steward of the organization's data assets? Conversations with most CIOs, however, yield a different result. CIOs are often the first to admit they do not have the requisite knowledge, skills and resources to do a good job in the data management area and that they spend most of their time and energy focused elsewhere. Managing information technology has been an all-consuming responsibility, leaving these talented individuals virtually no time or resources to manage organizational data.

Organizations should consider data management programs as something necessary and as common as having human resources programs to manage human assets.

SHARING DATA IN SOCIETY

Because society has not realized that data is truly an asset with virtually unlimited potential, there is no foundation on which society can grow future EDEs. The fact that organizations still have not realized that data is its most powerful and underutilized asset is startling. With very few exceptions, academic journals do not publish papers on the state of data management. Students do not study *data asset management.* Executives are not taught that organizational data management programs can produce ten-to-one returns on investment, both in terms of increased IT effectiveness as well as knowledge worker productivity. Some have noted that the EDE has fallen down the organizational ladder, reinforcing the idea that data management should occur in the basements of organizations and remain largely a technical discipline (Aiken & Gillenson, 2011). It is difficult to imagine things getting better with little education or research focused on this field.

LEVERAGING THE AGILE MANIFESTO FOR BUSINESS ACTIVITIES

The motivation to address system and societal challenges exist at all levels and comes from a common and correct perception that IT deliverables are overdue, more expensive than planned and lack promised functionality. Today, only 30 percent of projects are delivered on-time with full functionality and at the original price point. The larger the project, the greater its chances for failure (The Standish Group, 2016).

A general response has been to incorporate more *agility* (Koch, 2004) into these approaches to systems development as an:

[i]terative, incremental method of managing the design-and-build activities of engineering, information technology and other business areas that aim to provide new product or service development in a highly flexible and interactive manner.

Putting it simply, Agile provides valuable insight into complex projects that other methods cannot offer. This is especially true when requirements are fluid. During this process, an organization can direct user involvement and gather feedback at every step of the way. While many practices incorporate system users as development participants, they should also include those receiving and making downstream decisions based on the data. Consequently, it is worthwhile to contextually examine Agile and its successes before introducing data-centric thinking and the data doctrine. Because the data doctrine is in part an acknowledgement of the well-known, well-regarded and successful *Agile Manifesto* (Beck et al, 2001), this section will briefly review its premises.

No domain has benefitted more from Agile than software development. The dedicated professionals who have promoted Agile concepts deserve our collective thanks for truly advancing the state of the practice in this important area. We are confident that increasing organizational agility in the following areas will provide increased business value as well.

- communications
- governance
- data warehousing
- product management
- human resource management
- master data management

- project management
- construction

Ward Cunningham publicly posted the *Agile Manifesto* in 2001 to define an alternative to traditional documentation-driven software development processes. Signed by a critical mass of prominent software developers, the *Manifesto* presents some very important declarations, excerpts of which follow (Beck *et al*, 2001; see Figure 6.6).

We are uncovering better ways of developing software by doing it and helping others do it. Through this work, we have come to value

- individuals and interactions over processes and tools,
- working software over comprehensive documentation
- customer collaboration over contract negotiation and
- responding to change over following a plan.

That is, while there is value in the items on the right, we value the items on the left more.

Figure 6.6 Better ways of developing software

While widely adopted across industry and government, the signers were concerned that the overhead associated with software development was becoming unacceptably high—to the detriment of overall project success. Putting it simply, the signatories wanted to restore balance to their work (*ibid.*) and have clearly improved software development practices by doing so.

In many circumstances, Agile practices have proven to produce better quality software in shorter timeframes and with lower costs. In the following four subsections, we highlight the four premises behind the *Manifesto*.

Agile Premise No. 1: Value Individuals and Interactions Over Processes and Tools

There is no question the most difficult aspect of software development has always been understanding the requirements. If software and system requirements are flawed, inaccurate or incomplete, the product will suffer. As shown below, issues encountered in the earliest phases of software development cascade throughout the remainder of the development process and compound the cost to correct at each succeeding developmental step. Rather than slavishly following a specific method and producing mountains of documentation, Agile correctly suggests that projects should value actions that are used to better understand software requirements over rigid adherence to a process or original plan. Implicit in this assertion is the notion that no tool or method can "automagically" produce correct inputs to the development process unless the right people (*i.e.*, domain experts) are collaborating with software developers. Figure 6.7 shows just how critically important software requirements are to software development success (adapted from Davis, 1990 and Mizuno, 1983).

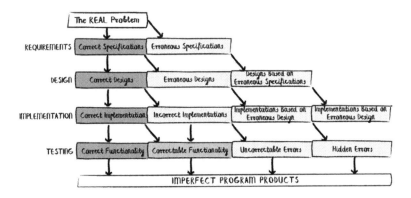

Figure 6.7 Cascading requirements are critically important to producing the desired software solution

Imagine attempting to implement everything that is incorporated in the figure but using wrong or otherwise imperfect data requirements. This would result in a lot of scrap and rework, assuming these data errors were caught during the development process. On many occasions, we have witnessed projects that did not identify data errors and, in other cases, projects simply papered over data errors with potentially unnecessary software functionality.

Agile Premise No. 2: Value Working Software Over Comprehensive Documentation

This Agile premise correctly asserts that having working software is more valuable than having documentation describing how software should work. As part of this premise, Agile methods shift emphasis from producing documentation to producing software substantiated through several prototypes and produced in tight collaboration with knowledge workers who are to use the software. This method has resulted in shorter feedback loops, more focused software builds and, often, less emphasis on computer-aided software engineering (CASE) tool methods used to manage software metadata.

Agile Premise No. 3: Value Customer Collaboration Over Contract Negotiation

What do you suppose would be the likelihood of your being able to accurately estimate how long work will take at the onset of a project, a time when you know the least about the work that must be done? Despite countless attempts to improve estimation techniques, software projects still suffer because of poor estimates. The Agile response to this was to de-emphasize attempts to predict precise price, schedule and functionality characteristics as contractual items. Instead, by collaborating with customers, understanding these items can be more quickly accomplished by accessing prototypes and works in progress rather than contract item negotiations. Agile has shown required software functionality can be delivered by a competent team, for a reasonable cost and within a satisfactory period if it has close customer cooperation.

Agile Premise No. 4: Value Responding to Change Over Following a Plan

Needless to say, understanding software requirements is immensely challenging. Add to this the fact that software complexity generally grows in direct relation to the size and complexity of the problem. Therefore, given a fixed plan with fixed budget, schedule and software functionality, organizations normally view changes as problematic and something that must be resisted. Agile has a different perspective: treating change not as a problem and failure of the original plan, but rather as improvement, refinement, clarification and enhancement to the original concept with each adding value to the project. To this end, Agile emphasizes need to adapt to change over up-front planning for each project.

Over time, the *Manifesto* has proven successful, inspiring a variety of approaches to software development that represent tangible, proven improvements over previous methods. Agile refocuses software development from rigid and mechanistic methods to more flexible and adaptive ones, particularly when there is uncertainty about system requirements. Agile is rightly considered to be an improvement to this aspect of systems development.

References

Aiken, P. & Billings, J. (2013). *Monetizing Data Management: Finding the Value in Your Organization's Most Important Asset.* Technics Publications.

Aiken, P. & Harbour, T. (2017, March). *Introducing the Data Doctrine.* Retrieved from http://www.datablueprint.com/introducing-the-data-doctrine.

Aiken, P., Gillenson, M., Zhang, X. & Raffner, D. (2011). *Data Management and Data Administration: Assessing 25 Years of Practice. Journal of Database Management* 22(3):24-44 July-September 2011.

Beck, K., Beedle, M., Van Bennekum, A. *et al.* (2001). *Manifesto for Agile Software Development.* Manifesto for Agile Software Development. N.p.

Chan, Y. E., Huff, S. L. & Copeland, D. G. (1997). *Assessing Realized Information Systems Strategy. The Journal of Strategic Information Systems,* 6(4), 273-298.

Chan, Y. E., Huff, S. L., Barclay, D. W. & Copeland, D. G. (1997). *Business Strategic Orientation, Information Systems Strategic Orientation and Strategic Alignment.* Information Systems Research, 8(2), 125-150.

Clarence, J. & Hempfield W. (2011). *Data Quality? That's IT's Problem, Not Mine: What Business Leaders Should Know about Data Quality.* Pittney Bowes Business Insights.

Eddy, D. (2011). *Repository Redux: Lessons Learned from 40 Years of Metadata Repositories.* The Fifth MIT Information Quality Industry Symposium (ISIQ) Proceedings 2011.

EDC Institute. (2016). *Building Global Interest in Data Literacy: A Dialogue,* 1–24. Massachusetts Institute of Technology (MIT) Economic Development Council (EDC).

Harris, H. & Murphy, S. (2013). *Analyzing the Analyzers: An Introspective Survey of Data Scientists and Their Work.* O'Reilly Media.

Keen, P. G. (1981). *Information Systems and Organizational Change.* Communications of the ACM, 24(1), 24-33.

Koch, A. (2004). *Agile Software Development* (pp. 1–303). Artech House, Inc.

Lattin, J. M. & Rierson, M. (2007). *Capital One: Leveraging Information-Based Marketing.* [M-316]. Case Studies and Teaching Materials. Stanford University.

Lippitt, M. (2003), *Leading Complex Change.* Enterprise Management, LTD.

Marr, B. (2015). *Where Big Data Projects Fail.* Forbes/Tech. http://bit.ly/2mTPOg1.

Morgan, J. (2016, May 26). *Manifesto for Data Management* [Letter to Peter Aiken].

Operating Principles. The IT Manager. ITMGRorg. N.p., n.d. Web. 15 Sept. 2016.

Porter, M. E. (2008). *Competitive Strategy: Techniques for Analyzing Industries and Competitors.* Simon and Schuster.

Project Management Institute (PMI). (2013). *A Guide to the Project Management Body of Knowledge* (PMBOK® Guide), Fifth Edition.

Sarsfield, S. (2009). *The Data Governance Imperative.* IT Governance Publishing.

The Data Doctrine. http://thedatadoctrine.com.

Tunguz, T. & Bien, F. (2016). *Winning with Data, Transform Your Culture, Empower Your People and Shape the Future.* John Wiley.

Vollmer, N. (2016, December 06). The EU General Data Protection Regulation. Retrieved from http://www.privacy-regulation.eu/en/r4.htm.

The Bottom Line:
A 3,000 Word Executive Summary

Chapter 1: Data Strategy Supports Organizational Strategy

Strategy acts as impetus for establishing organizational momentum and embodies the organization, and vice versa. The data strategy must embody the organization, and the organization must embrace the data strategy. Data strategy and data governance work together to ensure data assets fully support strategy. A good data strategy motivates usage of organizational data assets in support of an organizational strategy and specifies how data assets should be leveraged to support the organizational strategy.

Before beginning to develop a data strategy (Chapter 2), it is necessary to understand the relationship of data strategy to organizational strategy. Further, to understand what strategy is, it is important to understand the need for it. If the organization cannot execute its strategy, it will fail and likely cause substantial harm to the organization.

In today's digital world, the business becomes data and data becomes the business, and *the information derived from that data becomes a unique corporate asset.* An inventory of these organizational data assets is a necessary but insufficient prerequisite to implementing a successful data strategy.

Organizations must focus data strategies on those business outcomes that help the organization exploit data, creating value in the form of innovation, customer engagement and growth. A model for large organizations clearly illustrates the disconnect between organizational strategy and specific IT projects (see Figure 2.5 at page 65). Failure to align IT work with the organizational strategy results in problems, sometimes big problems.

Three fundamental elements constitute a viable strategy: analysis, choice and implementation. After analyzing the environment, organizations can identify basic business-level strategy choices that need to be made.

Assuming the organization to be largely aware of the "assetness" value of its various piles of data assets, the choice function is concerned with determining relative ability of data collections to produce information supporting the organizational strategy.

Employing data assets in support of organizational strategy has proven difficult for most organizations. Much of this can be categorized as a mismatch between projects and programs. Organizations implementing data strategy as a program (not a project) will succeed.

Chapter 2: Data Strategy Is Necessary for Effective Data Governance

The data strategy provides the *what,* and organizational data governance provides the *how* for organizations to achieve data goals. A strategy for data assets is necessary to provide a focus for effective data governance. The value of specific data increases as it is reused and focused on supporting organizational strategy. While organizations are often motivated to create a data strategy to improve data quality or increase data usage, there are three primary and more basic motivations for developing a data strategy.

- Improve your organizational data;

- improve your people's ability to use data; and

- improve people's ability to use data in support of strategy.

It is better to think of data as soil and not "the new oil." Differences in timing, valuation and reusability combine to make data unique among organizational assets.

Best also to be skeptical of the Big Data Technologies. The challenge now isn't the horsepower but instead is defining the business problem and only that should be driver for tool usage. Similarly require that your data scientists provide a third level of qualification on their data science credentials. Show us an actuarial data scientist, a health data scientist, a chemical data scientist, a weather data scientist, etc., and we can define knowledge, skills and abilities required to advance the field (a requisite for any science). Finally, we have yet to see a data science operation that feeds results of data munging operations back into production data as lessons learned about data quality, structure and operations.

While organizations long to exploit big data and perform advanced analytics, organizations need to realize that they must first crawl, then walk, then run relative with regard to data and, if organizations truly want to trust the results of computational abilities, they must be able to account for data across the entire data lifecycle—from acquisition through final disposition.

In summary, then, recent advances in data technologies (tools) have resulted in significant new ways of interacting with organizational data assets—despite the vagueness of the big data promise. In other words, big data technologies and industry specific data scientists can provide organizations some of the resources required to do more with data, but organizations still need a well-defined target and an understanding of where they are relative to that gap. This can be improved by recognizing that we need to teach more data management principles as part of core data science curricula and to partner data scientists with capable and qualified data management professionals.

It is necessary to determine which data collections house specific data items (where the data is), However, there is another unique aspect of data: data has a *combinatorial value* when it is combined with other data. As these companies have seen, the relative value of data explodes when it is combined with other data and, because most data today is "born digital," organizations have an opportunity to establish automatic links among data elements as each element is being created.

Because data is still understood to be a by-product of information technology, data continues to be defined in terms of software and systems development; organizations do not recognize data as being an ongoing process of environmental analysis, choice and adaptation.

Unless and until everyone is more data knowledgeable (has better educational background in data as an asset), organizations will not be able use data to support strategic initiatives. Before organizations can leverage data and enjoy its full value, organizations must first be confident in the quality the data.

As noted, such organizations have far-reaching problems that include an inability to leverage data assets, an incomplete inventory of enterprise data and duplicative data processing—among many others. Organizations must manage data like any other corporate asset, building the value of the data into return on investment (ROI) calculations.

Organizational benefits from this include the following.

- Greater understanding of organizational data holdings.

- Accurate accounting of organizational digital assets.

- Data strategy aligned to the overall organizational strategy.

- Value added to products and services.

- Enhanced customer experience.

- Transparency and efficiency.

- High-quality data that enables "more with less."

- Pressure from volume and velocity exerted on operating models and infrastructure.

Chapter 3: Data Strategy Development Phase I - Prerequisites

Organizations can begin to pursue the following goals based on the guidance described in Chapter 3.

- Establish data management knowledge, skills and abilities.
- Establish qualified hiring panels.
- Identify requirements for the organization's chief data officer.
- Remove barriers to data leveraging.
- Begin to think in a data-centric manner.
- Establish a programmatic way to share data.
- Establish protocols for orchestrating the data program with IT projects.
- Establish a process to sequence implementation of the data strategy.
- Recognize and address deeply-rooted organizational culture.
- Make an appropriate case for why data belongs to the business and not to IT.

The actions required to improve your data, the way your personnel use data and the way your organization uses data to support its strategy require a fundamental series of organization level changes that must be formally implemented and managed.

It is incumbent on organizations and leadership to ensure that all participants—and not just the data management team—increase the organization's data literacy and understand these principles to successfully leverage data.

Once understood, common organizational data needs can be maintained within the business part of the organization, and data management could provide well-defined data and data requirements to individual IT projects.

Led by the EDE, the organization needs to begin to develop corporate data management competencies in a series of chartered data management programs, projects and activities.

If organizations want to use data as a resource, they first must understand its dualistic nature; organizations will either leverage data in support of a business strategy or that same data will be an impediment. If organizations maintain an IT-centric approach to operations, EDEs will have to explain why data architecture and data management in general requires time to do and do well.

This chapter details specifics in three areas:

- **Lack of Organizational Readiness.** It is a big organizational change and must be formally addressed.

- **Unrecognized Lack of Qualified Talent.** Job titles and job requirements are immature and will gravitate towards value over time leaving immediate challenges for those desiring to hire.

- **Failure to Address the Seven Deadly Data Sins.** These sins prevent organizations from succeeding with data.

So, even though the organization has identified a way to get past lack of qualified data management leadership, the organization and the enterprise data executive (EDE) need to address and resolve the *Seven Deadly Data Sins* before attempting to develop smoothly running versions for its data strategy process. These data sins must be corrected in order to:

1) understands the underpinnings of data-centric thinking;

2) obtains qualified leadership for data initiatives;

3) separates data and software development;

4) sequences IT projects and the data program properly;

5) manages expectations;

6) sequences its data strategy appropriately; and

7) addresses cultural and change management aspects of data programs.

Chapter 4: Data Strategy Development Phase II - Iteration

Organizations can begin to pursue the following goals based on the guidance described in Chapter 4.

- Alignment of data strategy with organizational strategy.

- Development of a method to make iterative improvements to enhance organizational data management capabilities.

- Better understanding of the environment in which the organization operates.

- Establishment of a data vision that supports realization of organizational strategy.

- Better understanding of the impact vision will have on organizations.

- Establishment of a data management mission statement.

- Alignment of data vision and mission and with established business values.

- Establishment of objectives for a data strategy.

- Personnel who understand the data strategy.

This chapter focuses on the practical matter of producing a data strategy iteration, some of the obstacles that confront this work, what organizations should consider when producing data strategies and what should be included in documentation.

The ensuing collaborative project, that is, developing the data management strategy, is a powerful mechanism for clarifying executive actions and decisions and fast-tracking the data management program. All key players have had a voice; agreement is reached regarding objectives, priorities and measures; organization-level approval of capabilities to be improved is achieved; and all relevant stakeholders understand the impacts of the implementation sequence plan (Carnegie Mellon University, 2014).

You have prepared the organization for dramatic change, determined how to do the work, recruited qualified talent, eliminated the *Seven Deadly Data Sins* and have recruited a qualified, knowledgeable EDE to start developing a data strategy that the organization can implement.

An effective data strategy iteration addresses why the organization is implementing data management program feature and improvements.

Each iteration enhances the overall framework of the data management program and should be structured to address the core principles of data management so that critical stakeholders can understand the value of a data management program as it relates to functions and strategic initiatives.

It is important to note that, with each iteration of data strategy development, the organization should produce tangible business value and new organizational data capabilities.

The underlying method for accomplishing this has a long and rich history and many devotees. First outlined in the book, *The Goal*, the theory of constraints richly supports data strategy development and implementation. Organizations need to plan the introduction of data capabilities within organizational data strategies when they make sense and are understood by those who would be performing those duties. Repeated, absorbing the lessons, data strategy cycles give organizations the opportunity to improve a driving force within the organization.

Chapter 5: Data Strategy at Work

Several examples of Phase II data strategy development clarify some important aspects of the process.

One example discussed how absence of data strategy resulted in a dangerous combination of headline-making data breaches that culminated in the most serious threat to US national security in recent decades. A sound data strategy could have averted a national crisis resulting solely from a lack of understanding of the combinatorial value of data.

Others illustrated how three organizations each successfully incorporated data strategy and achieved tangible outcomes: the first used a solid framework to guide initial activities of a diverse team; the second illustrated how a logistics organization incorporated outcomes valuation as part of its data strategy; and the third demonstrated what had to be done to correct a misdiagnosed symptom.

Chapter 6: The Data Doctrine

This chapter introduces *The Data Doctrine* as supporting an understanding of data-centric thinking. With the completion of work described in this chapter, organizations can realize and monetize discrete and objective benefits.

- An understanding of the specifics involved in an objective means of verifying organizational practice of data-centric thinking.
- An understanding of the consequences of being a non-data-centric-thinking organization.

We consider the data doctrine necessary because, as described throughout this book, data programs are inherently and substantially different from software projects.

Lack of data education leads organizations to overlook the need for data programs and, instead, try to manage shared organizational data assets at the project level. There are some fundamental flaws with the process of incorporating data development into existing software development methods. These weaknesses can be summed up in a simple phrase: "The only way existing software projects can deliver effective results is when no data sharing occurs!" To derive the highest value from its data, an organization needs to position data as organizational assets and align them—along with other assets— to organizational strategic objectives. Organizations need to develop processes to support the collection of data provenance as well as data requirements before any work begins on software.

However, organizations have been infatuated with technology and the promised analytics that it delivers. As a result, they have often rushed past the inescapable fact that, if organizations do not have stable data, individual software projects will invent project-specific data and data structures.

This behavior is the force behind *dark data*, a kind of data ROT which Gartner defines as information assets that organizations collect, process and store during regular business activity but generally fail to use for other purposes (Tittel, 2016).

In the end, because data is more foundational than software, organizations must align data management strategy to organizational strategy before beginning software acquisition or iteration efforts. It is imperative to implement well-thought-out (i.e., engineered) data structures and strategy-supportive activities before acquiring software or developing new software capabilities. Finally, organizations should ensure that data architecture is flexible, adaptable and risk-adverse and that data be considered in coordination with software maintenance.

Index

Academic, 11, 54, 82, 85, 86, 87, 188, 196, 209
Accountability, 30
Accounting, 34, 59, 86, 167, 176, 221
Adams Media, 141
Adelman, Moss & Abai, 32
Affinity Diagram, 118
Agile development, 8, 164, 173, 189, 195, 203, 204, 209, 210, 212, 213, 214
Agile Manifesto, 195, 198, 203, 204, 211, 214
Agile Premise No. 1, 212
Agile Premise No. 2, 213
Agile Premise No. 3, 213
Agile Premise No. 4, 214
Agility, 8, 210
Aiken and Billings, 71, 92
Aiken and Gillenson, 92, 207
Aiken, P., i, 71, 92, 101, 108, 207
Algorithms, 55
Alignment, business and strategic, 5, 102, 106, 128, 194, 224
Analysis, 9, 20, 33, 34, 36, 54, 60, 62, 86, 95, 118, 131, 175, 185, 186
Analyst, 10, 32, 59, 129, 153, 154
Analytical phase, 89, 131
Architectural layer, 52
Architecture, 83, 85, 95, 97, 147
Artifact, 95, 166
Ashley Madison, 151, 158, 159

Association for Federal Information Resource Management (AFFIRM), 82
AT&T, 59
Attrition, 32
Audit, 182
Authority, 193
Balance sheet, 58, 59
Bandwidth, 29
Barclay, D.W., 102
Bargaining Power of Buyers, 38
Bargaining Power of Suppliers, 38
Barrier, 81, 82, 181, 222
Benefits, 32, 48, 59, 93, 115, 125, 135, 171, 174, 221, 226
Big Bang, 49
Big Data, 12, 52, 53, 54, 55, 61, 98, 192
    13 Vs, 53
    3 Vs, 53
BigOrganization, 37, 159, 160, 162, 165, 166, 172, 174
BigRetailer, 181, 182, 183, 184, 185, 186
Billings, J., 101
Blog, 138
Blue Ocean strategy, 35
Blueprint, 74, 105, 116, 144
Bonaparte, Napoleon, 24, 25, 36
Book librarian, 54
Booz Allen Hamilton, 4
Bottleneck, 120, 121, 122, 123, 182
Bottom line, 141
Brainstorming, 118

Broad differentiation strategy, 37
Broome, Lewis, 112
Budget, 116, 124, 139, 161, 165, 170, 171, 172, 173, 179, 185, 214
    Budget cycle, 165
Building block, 52
Business analyst, 182
Business case, 33, 171, 177
Business conversation, 40
Business data steward, 31, 32
Business environment, 8, 20, 27, 200
Business intelligence, 11, 62, 94
Business model, 3, 7
Business need, 130, 135
Business process, 10, 60, 85, 89, 94, 95, 112, 124, 132, 143, 162, 165
Business requirement, 8
Business rule, 72, 202
Business value, 5, 41, 67, 106, 116, 130, 131, 133, 167, 174, 210, 224
Business value realization, 67
Buytendijk, F., 192
Canada, 158
Capability, 5, 20, 34, 53, 65, 66, 82, 83, 84, 97, 98, 108, 110, 111, 117, 120, 127, 128, 130, 134, 144, 145, 147, 203, 224
Capability Maturity Model Integration (CMMI), 1, 82, 146
Capability Maturity Model Integration Data Management Maturity (CMMI/DMM), 82, 146

Capability Maturity Model Integration Institute (CMMI), 1
Capgemini, 61
Capital One, 99
Carnegie Hall, 98
Carnegie Mellon University, 106, 137, 194
Carroll, Linda, 1
Case study, 159
Cash flow acceleration, 32
Cause-and-Effect Diagram, 118
Cell phone, 17, 66
Certified Management Accountant (CMA), 86
Certified Public Accountant (CPA), 86
Chain (Goldratt system), 15, 55, 114
Chan, Y.E., 102
Change management, 76, 79, 82, 100, 171, 224
Change management process, 100
Characteristics, 28, 30, 48, 132, 156, 205, 213
Chartered Accountant (CA), 86
Chartered Certified Accountant (CCA), 86
Chartered data strategies, 79
Chief Data Officer (CDO), 1, 3, 6, 12, 14, 222
Chief Executive Officer (CEO), 3, 4, 137
Chief Financial Officer (CFO), 84, 86
Chief Information Officer (CIO), 77, 92, 208
China, 156
Chinese Whispers (Telephone Game), 140, 141, 142

Choice, 33, 36, 37, 38, 60, 105, 186
Clapper, James, 155
Clinton, Hillary, 62
Coca-Cola, 37
Collaboration, 43, 65, 112, 127, 213
Combinatorial value, 59, 151
Commitment, 39, 125, 134, 138, 172, 192, 193
Communication plan, 142, 164
Communications, 8, 16, 20, 21, 34, 80, 106, 128, 136, 137, 138, 139, 140, 141, 142, 163, 164, 171, 194, 210
Communications strategy, 137
Competetive content, 131
Competetive effectiveness, 32
Competition, 20, 21, 24, 34, 38, 67, 147
Competitor, 61, 89, 131
Computer, 5, 17, 34, 54, 136, 155, 156, 201, 203, 213
Computer information system, 34
Computer science, 5, 201
Computer-aided software engineering (CASE), 213
Computing platform, 66
Conference, 138
Constraint identification, 117
Constraint management, 116, 117, 123, 124
Constraint management processes, 116, 123, 124
Constraint maximization framework, 113
Constraints, 104, 113, 114, 115, 116, 117, 119, 120, 121, 122, 123, 124, 128, 177, 181, 182, 183, 184, 185
Constrating management planning, 116, 117, 124

Consumer, 1, 36, 64
Consumer Financial Protection Bureau, 1
Consumer preference, 64
Content ecosystem, 131
Content life cycle, 131
Content operations, 131
Content strategist, 131
Contract negotiation, 213
Contrator, 156
Copeland, D.G., 102
Core competency, 35
Core concept, 82
Core values, 133, 134
Corporate assets, 4, 39, 67
Corporate culture, 9, 26, 134
Cost containment, 32
Costs, 9, 16, 19, 24, 25, 26, 32, 35, 37, 50, 61, 83, 87, 99, 109, 116, 124, 174, 175, 176, 177, 183, 184, 185, 186, 191, 202, 206, 211, 212, 214
Credit card, 152
Critical path, 62
Cultural change management, 63
Cultural resistance, 75
Culture, 6, 34, 80, 100, 106, 115, 131, 164, 222
Cunningham, Ward, 211
Current information state, 132
Customer conversion, 32
Customer engagement, 7, 29, 40
Customer relationship management, 11
Customer request, 136
Customer service, 8, 32, 129, 133
Customer-centric, 8
Daniell, M., 19, 105
Dark data, 191
Data analytics, 4, 61

Data architecture, 94, 95, 97, 160, 195

Data architecture management, 94

Data asset management, 209

Data assets, 11, 12, 13, 29, 30, 36, 38, 41, 48, 49, 51, 57, 58, 59, 60, 64, 80, 83, 85, 90, 91, 92, 95, 104, 105, 111, 146, 161, 188, 195, 198, 208, 209, 217

Data breach, 151, 157, 159

Data challenge, 11, 47, 55, 112

Data classification, 42

Data collection, 36, 38, 57, 152

Data consistency, 160

Data consumer, 10

Data definition, 192

Data development, 94, 200

Data dictionary, 16

Data Doctrine, 188, 189, 197, 210

Data education, 60, 189

Data engineer, 92, 178

Data engineering artifact, 92

Data evolution, 204

Data flaws, 213

Data governance, 1, 30, 31, 41, 47, 56, 94, 145, 146, 160, 161, 162, 185, 192, 205, 217, 218

Data governance council, 161, 162

Data holdings, 18, 60, 62, 221

Data initiative, 81, 91, 95, 223

Data integration, 8

Data interchange, 160

Data investments, 5

Data jurisdiction, 91

Data knowledge, 64

Data leadership, 75, 78, 84, 101

Data level, 65

Data life cycle, 43, 98, 127

Data literacy, 10, 14, 15, 83

Data management, 1, 4, 55, 61, 64, 71, 73, 76, 77, 83, 85, 87, 88, 90, 92, 94, 95, 97, 98, 100, 101, 105, 109, 111, 116, 124, 125, 127, 144, 145, 146, 147, 160, 166, 170, 176, 178, 182, 198, 208, 209, 222, 224

Data Management Association (DAMA), 77, 82, 93

Data Management Association's Body of Knowledge (DMBOK), 93

Data management capabilities assessment, 166, 170

Data management framework, 125

Data management initiative, 97

Data management maturity, 82, 110, 144, 145, 146, 147

Data management maturity framework, 145, 146

Data management practices, 77, 83, 100, 124, 145

Data management professionals, 55, 83, 94

Data management programs, 97, 105, 111, 117, 125, 127, 198

Data manager, 4, 8, 77

Data maturity, 8, 14, 108, 110, 145

Data monetization, 67

Data needs, 90, 95, 173, 205

Data normalization, 8

Data operations, 145, 146

Data ownership, 71

Data planning, 108

Data planning components, 108

Data platform/architecture, 145

Data practice, 12, 160

Data practitioner, 83

Data prioritization, 43

Data product, 15, 16, 63

Data professional, 2, 5, 82, 87

Data program, 189, 190, 198, 200

Data provenance, 205

Data quality, 2, 8, 18, 31, 32, 55, 91, 94, 127, 145

Data quality management, 94

Data quality solutions, 2

Data quality steward, 32

Data requirement, 83, 87, 89, 90, 92, 95, 205, 213

Data revolution, 4

Data ROT (redundant, obsolete or trivial), 47, 56, 60, 191, 195

Data sandwich, 15

Data science, 5, 7, 54, 55, 98

Data scientist, 4, 9, 12, 48, 54, 55, 56

Data security, 13, 42, 43, 94

Data security collaboration, 42

Data security solution, 43

Data sharing, 66, 95, 200, 207

Data Sin, 82, 84, 87, 90, 91, 96, 98, 100, 101

Data standard, 92

Data steward, 31

Data strategy, 4, 5, 6, 7, 8, 9, 10, 12, 13, 19, 20, 27, 28, 29, 30, 31, 32, 36, 39, 40, 41, 42, 43, 47, 48, 49, 56, 64, 71, 72, 73, 74, 75, 78, 80, 81, 82, 84, 98, 99, 101, 103, 104, 105, 106, 108, 109, 110, 111, 112, 116, 117, 125, 126, 127, 128, 129, 130, 131, 132, 133, 136,

140, 142, 144, 145, 147, 151, 160, 161, 162, 163, 164, 165, 167, 169, 170, 171, 173, 174, 184, 185, 186, 192, 193, 194, 195, 196, 217, 218, 221, 222, 223, 224

Data strategy development, 56, 71, 129, 163, 173, 192, 193, 221

Data strategy development process, 129, 173, 193

Data strategy documentation, 164

Data strategy implementation, 98

Data strategy iteration, 104

Data strategy mission statement, 132, 133

Data strategy prerequisites, 73

Data strategy scope, 144

Data strategy support, 19, 41, 73, 217

Data strategy team, 161, 166, 167, 169, 170, 171, 173

Data structure, 195, 200, 201, 202, 203, 204, 205

Data structure requirements, 201

Data supply chains, 15

Data vision, 131, 161, 162, 171, 224

Data warehousing, 3, 11, 94, 145, 210

Data waste, 95

Database, 77, 94, 159, 177, 201, 202

Database operations, 94

Data-based strategies, 98

Data-centric, 29, 72, 81, 82, 94, 95, 96, 144, 160, 188, 189, 191, 195, 196, 197, 198, 200, 204, 205, 208, 210, 222, 223, 226

Data-centric development, 72, 197
Data-centric model, 96
Data-centric thinking, 81, 82, 94, 144, 188, 189, 191, 196, 197, 208, 210, 223
Data-driven, 4, 6, 11, 161
Data-focused, 80, 84
Datum, 51
Deadline, 33, 134, 163
Decision making, 32, 168
Degrade, 28, 30
Deliverables, 129, 132, 144, 163, 209
Demand chain management, 32
Demographics, 34, 152
Department of Homeland Security (DHS), 156
Dependency, 52
Deplete, 28, 30
Design principles, 204
Design-center, 8
Desired end state, 132
Desired information state, 131, 132
Dettmer, Michael, 120
Development, 14, 34, 60, 67, 77, 87, 90, 94, 107, 113, 127, 133, 178, 195, 197, 204, 210, 211, 212, 213, 214, 224
Deviation, 62
Digital, 4, 6, 7, 28, 29, 39, 60, 61, 63, 67, 221
Digital landscape, 29, 40
Digital mapping, 63
Digital networks, 61
Digital strategy, 127
Digital technology, 67
Digital transformation, 6, 7
Directives, 66
Director of National Intelligence, 155

Discovery, assessment, and current-state phase, 131
Discrete transaction, 58
Divide and conquer, 36
Document and content management, 94
Documentation, 31, 103, 107, 146, 203, 205, 211, 212, 213
Dodge, 24
Dollar General, 35
Domain data stewards, 31
Duggar, Josh, 158
Durable, 28, 30
Eckerson, 92
Economy, 4, 34, 49
Ecosystem, 40, 131
Eddy, David, 198
Education, 14, 48, 60, 76, 78, 87, 100, 135, 171
Efficiency, 16, 121, 221
Electronic format, 50
Electronic library, 194
Elevating, 104, 122, 186
Elevation improvements, 122
Eliyahu, M. Goldratt, 113
E-mail, 138, 158
Employee empowerment, 32
Employee engagement, 115, 138
Employees, 3, 26, 32, 66, 89, 115, 126, 138, 156, 157, 193, 202
Engineering, iii, 10, 83, 85, 201, 210
Enterprise data executive (EDE), 13, 80, 84, 85, 87, 92, 96, 97, 100, 101, 103, 106, 127, 162, 163, 164
Enterprise plan, 7
Enterprise policies, 6, 15
Enterprise solutions, 162
Environment, 8, 27, 32, 34, 36, 39, 40, 61, 63, 65, 119, 130,

131, 132, 161, 164, 168, 169, 192, 224

Environmental consideration, 136

Ernst & Young, 4

Estimates, 154, 156, 171, 175, 193, 213

Examples, 6, 11, 12, 17, 23, 24, 25, 32, 34, 58, 59, 62, 63, 66, 67, 79, 83, 84, 90, 99, 101, 109, 120, 121, 122, 127, 130, 133, 141, 151, 159, 160, 176, 181, 182, 184, 201, 202, 203, 204

Executive sponsorship, 100

Expectations, 3, 81, 84, 96, 97, 98, 129, 162, 166, 193, 224

Expenses, 50, 100, 161, 186

Exploit, 29, 35, 40, 66, 98, 104, 120, 121

Exploiting, 120, 184

Facebook, 48, 66

Fact, 18, 50, 51, 59, 60, 76, 109, 117, 120, 189, 205

Faria, Mario, 75

Federal Bureau of Investigation (FBI), 156

Federal government, 156

Feedback, 1, 92, 129, 210, 213

Finance, 34, 49, 86

Financial assets, 86

Fingerprints, 156, 157

Five Focusing Steps, 115

Flow, 13, 118, 201

Flow charts, 118

Focus, 3, 5, 21, 25, 29, 30, 31, 32, 37, 38, 40, 54, 56, 65, 72, 76, 90, 95, 103, 104, 112, 137, 143, 161, 162, 166, 169, 170, 182, 185, 186, 189, 195, 198

Focus groups, 166

Focused differentiation strategy, 37

Focused low-cost strategy, 37

Forrester Research, 14, 59

Foundation, 4, 52, 82, 83, 85, 131, 194

Foundational data management practice areas, 145

Foundational knowledge, 84

Fraud reduction, 32

Future-focused communication, 139

Future-state model, 131

Gaps, 5, 14, 56, 67, 83, 85, 118, 131, 166

Gartner, 4, 54, 75, 191

Gendron, Michael, 118

General Electric, 137

Generic business-level strategies, 36

Goals, 5, 19, 21, 22, 23, 24, 25, 26, 27, 28, 56, 73, 88, 95, 97, 100, 106, 114, 115, 118, 121, 123, 125, 126, 131, 139, 146, 161, 162, 165, 166, 168, 171, 173, 178, 179, 184, 221, 224

Goldratt, E. M., 113, 114, 116, 120, 177

Google, 49, 196

Governance, 30, 31, 48, 56, 104, 125, 126, 131, 210

Governance structures, 131

Governments, 9, 34, 130, 156, 159, 211

Graham, Friend and Stefan Zehle, 118

Gretzky, Wayne, 23, 34, 38

Grünig & Kühn, 36

Grünig, R., 107, 132, 192

Guidelines, 107, 133, 136, 179, 194

Hacks, 156

Harris, H., 54, 98
Hempfield, W., 92
Hidden data factory, 55
Hierarchical database
    management system, 177
High-level sequence plan, 125
Hubbard, Douglas W., 176
Hubble, Maggie, 1
Huff, S. L., 102
Human resource management,
    210
Human Resources, 20, 210
Humby, Clive, 49
Humphrey, Albert, 118
Hype cycle, 54
IBM, 14, 15
Impact, 49, 71, 132, 138, 203,
    224
Implementation, 30, 33, 38,
    48, 49, 64, 73, 95, 104, 126,
    128, 130, 207, 222
Incidental, ii
Information, ii, iii, 3, 4, 6, 10,
    15, 17, 18, 30, 34, 36, 39, 41,
    50, 51, 57, 58, 60, 64, 65, 77,
    83, 85, 89, 92, 94, 96, 100,
    102, 108, 128, 132, 137, 141,
    152, 154, 155, 156, 157, 158,
    159, 165, 166, 168, 171, 176,
    183, 191, 194, 197, 201, 203,
    208, 210
Information management
    competencies, 41
Information reuse, 51
Information Technology (IT),
    3, 4, 6, 9, 10, 18, 29, 40, 41,
    42, 58, 60, 65, 71, 72, 75, 77,
    81, 83, 84, 85, 87, 88, 89, 90,
    91, 92, 94, 95, 97, 98, 100,
    108, 110, 112, 137, 140, 141,
    142, 143, 174, 183, 184, 185,
    190, 191, 192, 194, 197, 207,
    208, 209, 210, 222, 223

Information Technology (IT)
    environment, 207
Information Technology (IT)
    projects, 9, 41, 65, 81, 87,
    88, 89, 90, 91, 92, 94, 95, 98,
    142, 143, 185, 222, 223
Information Technology (IT)
    security, 43
Information Technology (IT)
    systems, 3, 92, 96, 183, 184,
    197
Infrastructure, 58
Initiatives, 19, 56, 64, 75, 76,
    82, 97, 117, 118, 126, 130,
    160, 166, 169, 170, 173, 183
In-person events, 137
Inspiration, 20, 197
Intellectual property, 59
Intelligence, 50, 51
Internal and external publics,
    139
International Association for
    Information and Data
    Quality (IAIDQ), 82
International Shareholder
    Services (ISS), 152
International Society of Chief
    Data Officers (ISCDO), 83
Internet, 22, 66
Intranet, 138
Inventory, 13, 18, 115, 183
Investment, 4, 7, 8, 12, 29, 50,
    57, 67, 86, 98, 100, 115, 120,
    122, 147, 174, 185, 209
IT-centric, 97
Iterations, 49, 74, 104, 112,
    117, 159, 163, 185, 186, 193,
    204
Iterative, 104, 111, 113, 117,
    210, 224
IT-focused, 84, 95
iTunes, 66
Johnson, Gerry, 137

Johnson, Spencer, 63
Key performance indicator
(KPI), 62, 167
KeyPoint Government
Solutions, 156
Kirby, Michael, 2
Knowledge base, 85
Knowledge, skills and abilities
(KSA), 49, 76, 80
Kroes, Neelie, 49
Kroger Co., 63
Kundra, Vivek, 67
Ladley, 30
Laney, Doug, 12, 53
Lankford, David, 1
Latif, 193
Law, 34, 47
Lead times, 115
Leadership, 10, 11, 14, 20, 67,
73, 76, 81, 83, 85, 87, 90,
101, 104, 105, 142, 161, 167,
172, 193, 208, 223
Lean supply chain, 99
Legacy, 11, 12, 17, 18, 49, 177
Legal requirements, 136
Liddell and Scott, 22
Lifecycle, 191
Limitations, 117
Lippitt, Mary, 79
Loyalty card, 63
Magretta, 21
Manage change, 61, 62
Management, 11, 30, 34, 57,
73, 77, 83, 85, 87, 91, 92, 93,
94, 97, 99, 100, 107, 112,
114, 116, 124, 127, 128, 133,
134, 137, 144, 146, 160, 166,
177, 192, 193, 209, 224
Managing complex change, 79
Managing data, 8, 30, 145
Market, 4, 33, 34, 37, 38, 50,
61, 88, 99, 109, 130, 132,
135

Market demand, 130, 135
Market value, 4
Marketing, 32, 34, 62, 64, 155,
158, 171
Marketing effectiveness, 32
Marketplace, 21, 62, 160
Marr, 98
Marx, Gary, 137, 138
Mass media, 138
Massachusetts Institute of
Technology (MIT), 4
Master data management, 11,
109, 145, 210
Master file, 179, 180
Master of Business
Administration (MBA), 84,
86
Master of Science (MS), 86
Master plan, 74, 105, 116, 144
Mature, 7, 74, 84, 86, 98, 100,
105, 117, 164
Maturing, 144
McKinsey, 4, 10
McQuaig, 118
Meaning, 51, 130, 136, 179
Measure change, 61
Mecca, Melanie, 1
Media, 66, 138, 139, 158
Meetings, 3, 39, 137, 139, 164,
167, 169, 170
Merger and Acquisition, 8
Merriam Webster, 126
Metadata, 31, 57, 58, 92, 94,
96, 130, 205, 213
Metadata management, 57, 94,
205
Metadata repository, 130
Metadata reuse, 96
Methodology, 59, 87
Metrics, 67, 161, 167, 171, 182
Milestones, 62, 132, 163
Mining, 145, 177, 178, 179, 180

Mission, 13, 20, 21, 35, 67, 126, 132, 133, 134, 136, 140, 224
Mission statement, 132, 133, 224
Mobile computing, 66
Mobile devices, 60
Moonlighting, 202
Motivate change, 48, 61, 63
Motivation, 21, 28, 56, 60, 64, 140, 209, 217
Multi-voting, 118
National security, 66, 152, 159
Nestlé SA, 64
Networks, 40, 114
New York Times, 156
Niche strategy, 37
Nominal Group Technique, 118
Non-governmental organization (NGO), 9
Obama, Barak, 62
Objectives, 5, 12, 16, 19, 21, 22, 27, 28, 53, 59, 95, 97, 106, 111, 116, 118, 123, 125, 126, 127, 129, 133, 134, 135, 136, 139, 160, 161, 162, 165, 166, 167, 168, 170, 171, 173, 224, 226
Observations, 34, 53
Obsolete, 47, 185
Oceans of Data Institute/Education Development Center (ODC/EDC), 14
Office of Personnel Management (OPM), 151, 155, 156, 159
Office of Personnel Management (OPM) data breach, 156
Office of the Director of National Intelligence (ODNI), 155

Operational data stewards, 32
Operational environment, 36
Operations, 9, 27, 33, 34, 55, 73, 98, 99, 105, 135
Opportunities, 5, 7, 8, 41, 60, 86, 118, 131, 166, 170
Optimization, 113, 179
Organizational agility, 210
Organizational climate, 79
Organizational data, 12, 15, 28, 30, 41, 42, 47, 48, 49, 55, 56, 59, 60, 73, 87, 90, 91, 92, 95, 99, 104, 108, 162, 181, 189, 209, 217, 224
Organizational data maturity, 108
Organizational data needs, 90, 92
Organizational data strategy, 41, 47, 73, 108
Organizational fortitude, 39
Organizational inertia, 79
Organizational knowledge, 41
Organizational needs, 108, 111, 129, 174
Organizational policy, 14, 73, 127
Organizational productivity, 55
Organizational readiness, 74, 223
Organizational requirements, 90
Organizational strategy, 14, 19, 25, 28, 29, 30, 33, 38, 40, 41, 42, 48, 64, 67, 74, 78, 80, 94, 95, 99, 104, 105, 106, 108, 112, 117, 127, 131, 140, 141, 142, 143, 161, 162, 163, 184, 195, 198, 217, 221, 224
Organizational transformation, 62
Organizational units, 142, 192

Organizations consideration formula, 131
Pahl & Richter, 118
Pareto, 47, 118
Pareto analysis, 118
Parker and Mattia, 203
Patton, General George S., 21
People, process, policy and technology (P3T), 29, 54, 58, 64, 65, 74, 109, 161, 167, 171
Performance, 62, 67, 87, 109, 114, 123, 129, 132, 134, 172, 182, 183
Person-century, 174
Person-year, 180
Phase I, 71, 73, 76, 104, 151, 162, 221
Phase II, 73, 76, 104, 151, 162
Plans, 5, 14, 22, 23, 36, 39, 67, 86, 92, 100, 104, 105, 110, 116, 117, 119, 124, 126, 127, 135, 137, 139, 140, 142, 144, 145, 161, 162, 163, 164, 165, 166, 167, 168, 169, 170, 171, 173, 184, 214
Platform, 147
Point of diminishing returns, 174, 177
Policy, 1, 29, 30, 54, 66, 122, 126, 139, 181, 194
Politics, 34
Porter, William, 98
Portfolio, 87, 106
Powell, Linda, 1
Practice year, 130
Pregnancy, 154
Pregnancy prediction, 154
Pregnant, 155
Prerequisites, 13, 71, 73, 74, 96, 101, 103, 145
Principle, 55, 83, 85, 106, 112, 117, 133, 142, 160

Priorities, 5, 13, 105, 125, 126, 127, 160, 168, 170, 185, 186
Process, 7, 10, 15, 21, 29, 33, 50, 53, 54, 55, 57, 59, 60, 66, 77, 78, 92, 96, 101, 104, 105, 108, 110, 111, 114, 115, 116, 118, 121, 122, 123, 124, 125, 127, 132, 134, 139, 140, 141, 144, 145, 162, 163, 164, 165, 166, 167, 170, 171, 173, 175, 177, 178, 179, 180, 181, 183, 184, 185, 191, 193, 196, 200, 204, 205, 210, 211, 212, 213, 222
Process design, 175
Process maps, 118, 175
Procter & Gamble Co., 64
Product management, 8, 210
Product scope, 126
Production, 17, 34, 55, 87, 120, 121, 122, 129
Product-use cycle, 50
Profitability, 86, 115, 132, 185
Program, ii, 4, 5, 7, 30, 48, 54, 56, 64, 65, 67, 71, 76, 81, 82, 84, 85, 91, 93, 105, 106, 111, 116, 127, 135, 139, 144, 169, 170, 173, 201, 204, 209, 222, 223, 224
Program managers, 106
Programmatic, 67, 74, 87, 95, 104, 183, 199, 204, 222
Project, 15, 31, 62, 64, 65, 67, 77, 83, 87, 88, 89, 90, 91, 92, 94, 106, 109, 112, 124, 126, 129, 130, 134, 135, 136, 143, 171, 179, 180, 189, 192, 198, 200, 204, 206, 209, 210, 211, 213
Project data stewards, 31
Project management, 62, 67, 91, 106, 124, 126, 211

Project Management Institute
(PMI), 67, 91, 106, 124, 126
Project scope, 126
Project sponsors, 106
Project value, 180
Promulgation, 194
Prototype, 213
Prussians, 25, 36
Public Relations, 32
Public sector, 21, 130
Purchases, 58, 122, 154
Purpose, 19, 35, 49, 57, 117,
125, 126, 134, 140, 145, 191
Qualified talent, 74, 223
Quality, 21, 32, 48, 56, 64, 91,
96, 100, 115, 120, 133, 140,
147, 160, 161, 178, 191, 195,
211, 221
Quality management, 100
Quality management
initiatives, 100
Quebec, 158
RACI matrix, 118
Rall, Ted, 175
Raw data, 57
Record-keeping, 86, 120
Redman, Thomas C., 2
Redundant, 47, 54, 185, 191
Reengineer, 181, 183, 185
Reference and master data
management, 94
Registered users, 158
Regulations, 66, 181
Regulatory requirements, 130
Reputation, 33
Requests, 51
Research, 1, 34, 49, 54, 77, 85,
102, 128
Resource needs, 170
Resources, 5, 11, 12, 14, 16, 18,
21, 56, 62, 76, 84, 97, 107,
120, 121, 124, 133, 140, 143,

163, 165, 170, 181, 183, 190,
191, 200, 208
Retention, 32
Return on Assets (ROA), 4
Return on Investment (ROI),
4, 8, 67, 163, 167, 168, 169,
171
Reusable code, 205
Reusable data, 72
Reuse, 28, 50, 85, 95, 195, 198,
199, 204, 205
Revenue, 7, 32, 61, 182, 183,
184
Revenue enhancement, 32
Ripple effects, 204
Risks, 16, 43, 57, 58, 100, 110,
171
Ritter, Christopher, 1
Roadshows, 138
Root-cause analysis, 118
Sacks, Jonathan, 110
SAS Business Series, 59
Scholes, Kevan, 137
Scope, 27, 77, 92, 125, 126, 147
Scorecards, 62, 118
Security clearance, 156, 157,
159
Segmentation, 36
Seven Deadly Data Sins, 74,
81, 101, 103, 223
Shared data, 88, 189, 198, 203,
204
Shared resource, 198
Sheena (Example), 175, 176
Short-term goals, 33
Siegel, Eric, 54
Sinek, Simon, 20
SIPOC Diagram, 118
Smallword, Robert, 198
Smith, Ray, 1
Social environment, 66
Social need, 135
Social networks, 58

Society, 34, 139, 188, 209
SOFT Model, 118
Software applications, 66, 94
Software code, 198, 200
Software coding, 31, 182, 195, 198, 200, 204
Software complexity, 214
Software development, 81, 83, 189, 195, 197, 200, 210, 211, 212, 214, 223
Software program, 201, 203
Software projects, 198, 199, 200, 203, 204, 205, 213, 214
Software requirements, 212, 214
Sports Illustrated, 23
Stakeholders, 75, 112, 117, 126, 127, 128, 129, 130, 132, 136, 137, 139, 144, 163, 165, 166, 167, 169, 170, 171, 172, 173, 193
Standards, 15, 16, 59, 65, 85, 126, 145, 146, 160, 185, 188, 194, 196
Stanford University, 118
Statistics, 54, 182
Stock-keeping units (SKUs), 177, 179, 180
Store numbers, 182, 183
store-id, 182, 183, 184, 185, 186
Stories, 136, 151
Storytelling, 136, 165, 173
Strategic analysis, 35
Strategic choices, 37, 98
Strategic control, 107
Strategic documents, 192
Strategic objectives, 41, 51, 142, 143, 166, 199
Strategic opportunity, 135
Strategic planning, 107, 133, 162, 166, 170, 192
Strategic value, 199

Strategies, 4, 5, 6, 7, 10, 11, 12, 13, 19, 20, 21, 22, 23, 24, 25, 26, 27, 28, 29, 30, 33, 34, 35, 36, 37, 38, 39, 41, 42, 47, 48, 49, 50, 56, 64, 67, 73, 74, 75, 82, 86, 94, 97, 100, 102, 103, 104, 105, 106, 107, 109, 112, 113, 116, 118, 125, 127, 128, 129, 131, 133, 134, 136, 137, 138, 140, 141, 142, 143, 144, 147, 161, 162, 163, 164, 165, 166, 167, 169, 170, 171, 172, 173, 186, 189, 192, 193, 195, 217
Strategy development, 107, 129, 140, 172
Strategy failure, 24, 25, 26
Strategy implementation, 107
Strategy management, 106
Straw man, 169
Strengths, 98, 113, 114, 117, 118, 131
Strengths, Weaknesses, Opportunities, and Threats (SWOT), 118
Supreme Court Justice Potter Stewart, 53
Swim-lanes, 39
Syntax, 198, 201
System constraints, 104, 117, 120, 122, 124, 184
Tabular data, 177
Target, 151, 152, 154, 156, 159
Technical architecture, 7
Technical data stewards, 31
Technological advances, 136
Technology, 5, 7, 11, 18, 20, 29, 34, 41, 47, 49, 86, 88, 94, 100, 105, 110, 126, 136, 166, 170, 191, 192, 205, 208
Technology advisory council, 170
Technology initiatives, 11, 166

TED Talks, 20
Telephone, 141
Tesla, 109
The Standish Group, 209
Theory of Constraints, 113, 115, 116, 128
Threat of new entrants, 38
Threat of substitute products, 38
Tittel, Ed, 192
Toyota, 37
Tradeoffs, 36, 37
Training, 86, 87, 100, 122, 129, 135, 139, 171, 193
Transactional data, 58
Transparency, 77, 221
Trivial, 10, 47, 59, 184, 185
Twitter, 66
U.S. Chief Technology Officer, 1
U.S. Presidential election, 62
Unicorn, 80
United Airlines, 48
United States, 152, 155, 159
United States Investigation Service (USIS), 155
User, 166, 173, 210
User stories, 166, 173
Valuable, 4, 50, 53, 57, 58, 59, 61, 67, 112, 146, 160, 210, 213
Value, 4, 7, 11, 13, 15, 19, 28, 29, 30, 34, 39, 41, 48, 49, 50, 55, 57, 58, 59, 61, 64, 67, 87, 97, 98, 100, 101, 112, 117, 120, 130, 134, 165, 173, 176, 177, 180, 189, 191, 194, 198, 199, 205, 212, 213, 214, 221
VANITY, 53
Velocity, 12, 53, 123, 221
Vendor, 130, 182
Video, 138
Vision, 5, 19, 67, 100, 125, 131, 132, 133, 134, 162, 166, 171, 172, 173, 224
Vision statement, 125
Vitamin supplements, 154
Vocabulary, 194
Voicemail, 138
Volume, 9, 12, 53, 92, 169, 221
Walmart, 25, 26, 35, 37
Waterloo, 24, 25
Weakest link, 114, 120, 122, 123, 145
Weaknesses, 98, 117, 118, 119, 200
Web applications, 66
WEBCPA, 86
Websites, 66, 139
Welch, Jack, 137
whitehouse.gov, 158
Whittington, Richard, 137
Who Moved My Cheese?, 63
Whole Foods, 35
Wikipedia, 23, 176
Williams, 33
Workgroups, 15, 160, 161, 162
Workload, 178
Workshops, 14, 137, 138, 162
YouTube, 66

71882933R00139

Made in the USA
Middletown, DE
01 May 2018